D10

COPING WITH

C000193111

Coping with BEREAVEMENT

Coming to terms with a sense of loss

SANDRA HORN

Thorsons Publishing Group

First published 1989

© Sandra Horn 1989

British Library Cataloguing in Publication Data.
Horn, Sandra, *1944–*
Coping with bereavement: coming to terms
with a sense of loss.
1. Bereavement & loss. Personal adjustment
I. Title
306.8'8

ISBN 0 7225 1651 7

Published by Thorsons Publishers Limited, Wellingborough,
Northamptonshire, NN8 2RQ.

Printed in Great Britain by
Woolnough Bookbinding Limited,
Irthlingborough, Northamptonshire

1 3 5 7 9 10 8 6 4 2

Contents

Acknowledgement

I am indebted to Catherine Dobson and the staff of the Royal Hampshire County Hospital Library in Winchester for a great deal of friendly help with references and addresses. *Bereavement counselling*, compiled by Catherine Dobson, has been an invaluable source book. I should also like to thank Hilary Haymes and other staff in the library of the Royal South Hants Hospital, Southampton, for their help in chasing references.

My good friend Joan Galbraith has cast her expert eye over some early drafts of the manuscript and given me the benefit of her wisdom and humour. Thank you, Joan.

Thanks and apologies to my family and friends for putting up with living with me and the book during the months of its gestation.

The biggest thank you of all to Mavis Whybrow, whose skill, patience and calm good humour have coped with multiple re-drafting, lost pages, my handwriting, and still come up trumps with the typing.

Introduction
Who are the bereaved?

In the usual meaning of the word 'bereaved', the loss is of another person, with whom there has been a close loving relationship, a person who has become a part of one's self. Sometimes it is a person not yet known, but who has existed in hopes and dreams, as when an unborn or tiny child dies. In this kind of loss, grief is tied to the event, it has a time to begin. Loss can also be experienced, however, of something or someone that never was. Infertility, for example, can give rise to a diffuse grief reaction; it may come and go with the hope of each pregnancy, and become more or less of a problem as years go by and hope fades. These losses take away that aspect of us which was or wanted to be a parent. Other aspects of the self, like brother or sister, child, husband, wife or friend can also be changed or taken away by death.

Bereavement can also be experienced as a result of other major life-changes involving exits or losses. For example, disability as the result of an accident or illness can also take away part of the self. There may be a literal removal or distortion of part or function of the body, involving complicated re-learning about that aspect of the self. This loss may also involve social roles such as wage earner, or personal feelings of competence, independence, wholeness. Many life-changes may be consequent upon such losses, requiring a lot of adaptation to regain a sense of being a complete person.

Bereavement can also be experienced when someone loses a job. It may have provided not only financial security, given a structure to the day, a certain place or role in the community, and friendship groups, but also part of our identity. 'What do you do?' must be one of the most common questions people ask when they meet someone new. It 'places' someone immediately;

it is a talking-point. Even at the most basic level, 'breadwinner' and 'wage earner' are proud words, and the demands a job makes on our skill and commitment are important aspects of self-esteem. Losing all that cannot fail to leave its mark. If the loss of the job happens late in life, or at retirement, the change may also incorporate fears for the future, and coming to terms with old age. Again, losses like these may require major re-adjustments in lifestyle and self-perception.

Other life-transitions, such as children leaving home, moving house, changing school or job, can produce periods of grief while the ache for the old familiar life is acute, and there is a struggle to adapt to the new. Old ties and habits can be strong, and letting them go is no easy matter, particularly when the new life seems to offer a raw deal, and one thrust upon you rather than freely chosen. There are times in the early days of such transitions when the strength and will to go on may seem to be lacking. 'What's the point?' is a common question; 'I can't see my way through this' is a common feeling.

Significant losses are experienced by increasing numbers of people as populations become more mobile. Travelling is relatively easy, all over the world. Arriving in a strange culture with an unfamiliar-looking landscape, new climate, strange language and customs, can produce all the shock, depression and difficulty commonly seen in other forms of bereavement, and can also demand major re-adjustment.

Thoughts like this, and many others full of fear and self-doubt, are common in the acute stages of grief after a major loss, and often persist for a long time. Sometimes, the passage of time and sheer necessity, get us through. Often help is needed, or the unresolved difficulties become a stumbling-block, and people 'stick' in their grief for years, or for the rest of their lives. In this way, the pain of loss becomes a permanent feature of life, rather than an experience from which we can learn. The disabled, unemployed, widowed, can sink into apathy if no way out is offered, and the road back from that is very hard indeed. We do now understand much about the process of grief, and how those in difficulties can be assisted through it. We can recognize that behaviour which is, on the surface, awkward or uncooperative, may be a clue to a very different state of mind. We have learned that grief has its time and place in various aspects of life; that to be bereaved is *not* the same as being neurotic; that grief does *not* need treatment aimed at suppressing it; that the best help for the bereaved is to be allowed to express and share and explore their feelings, and to be lovingly supported through the transition. We are all bereaved at some time or another, and will all have the opportunity to help one another's grief. As the old Chinese story says, we cannot prevent the bird of sorrow from flying round our heads, but we can stop it nesting in our hair.

1

Attitudes to death

Throughout history, and across cultures, man has invented theories about death, and has prescribed how people bereaved by death should behave and should be treated. There is wide variation in this, from extreme cruelty as in the suttee imposed on Indian widows, to compassionate provision as that practised in the old Jewish religion, where a widow was married by her husband's brother, thus being given a home and status. Most of these ideas have been based on cultural and religious beliefs, not on scientific methods of study of the bereaved. Like many other important life-events, bereavement and how to cope with it, has been left largely to chance. We do not teach it in schools. We know that people will not stumble across how to cope with arithmetic or reading by chance, but we expect that relationships and emotions can be learned like that, or that they will come 'naturally'.

Sometimes leaving life skills to chance pays off, sometimes it does not. If we are exposed to a variety of experiences when we are young, and can watch parents or other important adults handle them competently, we can learn from them. But if the experiences are not there (and loss by death is a rare thing for children to come across these days) or if we see other people not coping well, how can we learn to get it right? These things are too important to be left to chance; they may make the difference between a happy and successful life, and one full of pain and difficulty. A necessary first step in incorporating life skills into education is to gather information on what is helpful in a systematic way.

In western cultures, topics like bonding (ties of affection) and loss have recently become the subject of such studies, and patterns of thoughts, feelings and behaviour characteristic of

bereavement have been identified. We can now shed superstition and begin to use informed compassion. We can deal in
needs, not vague theories. In some areas of concern, this has
been slow to come, but thanks to the work of researchers such as
Bowlby and Murray Parkes, bereavement by death is now much
better understood. However, bereavement by loss of part of the
body or body function or the bereavement felt on redundancy
from work, for example, are only now beginning to be considered. Physical medicine and social policy have lagged behind
psychiatry and psychology in this respect. However, things are
beginning to change, and the role of grief and loss in medicine
and in other areas of life is being increasingly studied and
taught. We are beginning to listen, to observe, to give people
time to adjust, to use all our accumulated knowledge about how
we attach ourselves to people, places and things, why these
attachments are important, and what happens when they are
broken.

In some cultures, bereaved people are isolated for some days;
no one comes near them. The reasons for this are based on
superstition. We now understand that friendship and human
comfort are important after loss, to help the bereaved person
through a difficult time. We also know that reminiscence can
help people to bear the pain of loss and that memories are
precious.

The ancient Greeks believed that a dead soul had to forget all
it had known on earth in order to adjust to life in the hereafter. It
is an extraordinary idea. It probably comes from the notion that
memory of things past would be painful, and cause grief. It is
true that for a time after loss, memories can bring pain, but it is
also true that, in the end, the pain eases but the memories
remain. How awful it would be if this were not true. We build on
the past, learn from it, grow through it. 'The thought of our past
years in me doth breed perpetual benediction', wrote Words-
worth; he is talking about the memory of earlier affections,
which he says are the 'fountain light of all our day . . . a master
light of all our seeing', and which uphold and cherish us.
Nothing can take the influence of good things in the past away,
even if bereavement intervenes and changes the future. Close
attachments help to form us and, even if they break, they will
have done their vital work already.

Many of our human needs are supplied by people, places and
objects, to which we are attached, and much of our humanity is

expressed through the same attachments. From the earliest parent-child bonding, our need for attachment, and our gift for creating it, spread and grow, giving us a sense of belonging, of safety, and helping to define who we are and where we fit into the scheme of things. These are the *rewards* of attachment. The other side of the same coin is loss, or the possibility of loss. From our earliest years, we have to learn to deal with the fact that people and things change and leave us. We have, of course, the basic capacity to learn and adapt to loss, but it is often hard to use that capacity fully. Losses do not always occur conveniently, when we are at our strongest and most capable. The thinking, rational part of the brain cannot function at its best when it is overwhelmed by longing for the lost object, and by fear and grief. Losses are not always expected, so that they can be prepared for, and they are often complicated by tangled emotions. For all these reasons, someone adapting to loss often needs help.

The greatest potential sources of help available to anyone undergoing loss come from other people, and, for some, from a sense of something beyond our normal everyday experience, which makes sense of grief and adversity and offers consolation. That spiritual or religious dimension is mediated, however, by other people. By direct contact, or by reading of the experiences of others, we are sustained and helped through times of grief. We are each other's own best resource. Sadly, people are not always available to each other at these times. Because some kinds of loss are particularly difficult, they can have wide-reaching effects. They produce insecurity and feelings of threat, not only in the people undergoing the loss, but in others who know about it. 'Never send to know for whom the bell tolls; it tolls for thee', said Donne, and this message is true — there *is* a feeling that the bell announcing loss by death does toll for all of us. The result of that may be to bring people together to face the common threat and to comfort and help one another, or it may drive them apart, each wrapped up in their own fears. It is a great pity that this happens as there is everything to be gained by sharing in adversity, and much to be lost by shunning others at such times. Loss, particularly when it is caused by death, often has a great deal of fear attached to it, and it is usually then, when fear gets the upper hand, that the normal human desire for closeness breaks down.

The film director, Ingmar Bergman, once said that making *The*

Seventh Seal had exorcised his own fear of death. I can remember being afraid to go and watch it, many years ago. Why come deliberately face to face with something so awful when there was no need? It was a mistake I now find myself encouraging others not to make. Death may be a hard fact of life, but we make it more awful than we need to by turning away from it, trying to pretend it has nothing to do with us.

In the film, a knight journeying home encounters Death, and buys time by playing chess with him. On his travels, the knight passes through a land in the grip of plague; the fear of death is everywhere. He encounters a whole spectrum of human behaviour, from cruel religious excesses and superstition, to moral decay, as a result of the fear. He also meets some simple people who are not touched by this fear. Their love for each other and their child, and life itself with all its possibilities, surrounds and protects them. They recognize Death, but are not afraid of him and the fact of Death does not destroy their happiness. They are glad for what each day brings, and hopeful for the future. The knight learns from them that the fear of Death is more destructive than Death itself, and he is sustained and helped by their warmth, and the food they share with him.

There are, no doubt, deeper layers of meaning in the film, but the power of simple human love is central to it, as is the dark shadow cast by fear. It is natural to have some fear of the unknown, and to be afraid when someone or something important is taken away, but these fears are usually resolved with time and help. Fear becomes destructive when it cuts us off from each other. If we need to work harder at dealing with it today, it is because most of us do not encounter death until relatively late in life whereas in Victorian times, for example, it was a common event. Death is a common theme in Victorian literature, even for children. Children would encounter the loss of relatives (notably among their own age group; infant mortality was very high). Death was not only common, but it had a great deal of public ritual surrounding it, such as the wearing of mourning clothes, so that everyone would be aware, and would know how to behave. Nowadays, nothing marks the bereaved as being in a special state. Perhaps it is not surprising that embarrassment and social awkwardness so often accompany encounters with recently bereaved people — we are out of practice, as it were, even though we all know what loss feels like. Despite the fact that loss by death may not be common early in life, loss due to other causes is universal from our earliest years. This means that we can, in a sense, prepare for the greater losses through these smaller ones. We can certainly empathize with the bereaved, even when we have not had that particular kind of loss to deal with. By remembering other losses, by learning from books and other sources, and by having confidence in the power of kindness (nothing more complicated), the sorrow of others can be eased. This is not a one-way process, however. We grow from it and gain from it ourselves. It is also true that those who have suffered bereavement may be strengthened by it, if they are allowed to be, by circumstance and by others around them.

The dictionary defines *loss* in terms of deprivation, detriment, incurred disadvantage, to be the worse off . . . a loss is a thing we fail to obtain, cease to possess, become unable to find, a thing gone astray. All these ideas are full of sadness, and are universal, often-repeated human experiences. Yet we can look around and see that people are not bowed down with sorrow. Any one of us may be overcome by it for a while, and more than once, but the pain and loss does not go on, unchanged and forever. The human spirit has the ability to turn the experience of major loss into strength, can pick up the shattered pieces of what remains and build something new — something often stronger than what was there before.

Charles Dickens, together with many other authors, understood this well. All his heroic characters, with whom it is so easy to identify, have been tempered in the fires of loss and adversity. Towards the end of *David Copperfield*, for example, Agnes writes to assure him that he will gain a higher and firmer tendency through all the grief that he has undergone and that in him, sorrow could not be a weakness, but must be strength. She tells him that the things he had to endure in his early days played a part in making him what he is, and that what calamity has taught him, he could teach others. She is doubtless thinking that calamity has given him his mature wisdom, his patience, steadfastness and compassion. In sharp contrast, Dickens gives us a portrait of his 'childwife' Dora. She is disabled, not in body or mind, but in spirit and character. She has not been touched and formed by hard experiences, and so remains a 'soft' doll–like girl.

Even so, there is something appealing in the idea of a life free from any cares or troubles. Man has always, it seems, dreamed of fairyland, Utopia, a sort of heaven on earth, where the sun always shines, no tears fall, nothing changes or decays, nothing sad or bad obtrudes. The dream of a total absence of adversity and pain is pretty well universal, and quite extraordinary. How could a human being survive it? Nothing to challenge, nothing to overcome or strive for, no need for pity or compassion? It doesn't bear thinking about. Never-never land would be far more destructive of the human spirit than the losses and griefs each one of us encounters in the journey through life.

This is not to say that *all* losses can be used for the ultimate good. Sometimes they are overwhelming. Grief cannot always be resolved and the person who has suffered the loss can be disabled by it. There are a number of things which can tip the balance one way or the other; things which can turn grief into a learning and growing experience, or a life-long, unhealed wound.

In my work, I have often been allowed to share in someone else's grief. Recognizable patterns of feelings and behaviour sometimes emerge in the course of counselling someone struggling to come to terms with a significant loss, and it can be helpful to all concerned to understand these patterns. For example, in the rehabilitation of someone who has had a limb amputated or has lost a body function through a stroke or spinal injury, there are times to push on with physical therapy, and times to leave it while a particular stage of the grieving process is attended to. It is the same after any major loss, such as losing someone through death, or losing one's job. No intervention, no matter how well meant, can be effective if it comes at the wrong time in the mourning process.

Any significant change in life, particularly when it involves a loss or 'exit' of someone or something important, can trigger a grief reaction. Events which make us change long-established patterns of behaviour, including ideas and feelings about ourselves, are bound to produce a time of personal upheaval, the consequences of which can be disabling. This is particularly likely to be true when the change is unexpected, and has far-reaching effects, especially if the person it happens to lacks family or social support, or is left in poorer circumstances or with fewer reasonable options open. We know some of the answers to questions about the outcome of losses, and it can be shown that planning and management can exert a strong influence for the good on these difficult life-transitions. The process of adapting to loss, and mending the battered self so that life can go on, is understandably lengthy and difficult, more so for some people than for others. The more knowledge and understanding that can be brought to bear on it, the more suffering can be eased and adaptation enhanced.

2

Preparation

We cannot take away or 'cure' grief — nor should we want to. It occupies an essential place in everyone's life-story, just as joy does. However, an extra dimension of fear and anguish is often added to grieving because the prospect of death has not been faced, and we *can* avoid some of this unnecessary suffering by advance preparation. Perhaps this seems an odd idea at first, to prepare for death, but it is no more odd than planning for other parts of the future.

Even as recently as 50 years ago, hardly anyone would have grown to adulthood without experiencing the deaths of people close to them. Today we regard such early experiences as unusual, tragic misfortunes. Social and medical advances have taken away our familiarity with death and most people do not expect to lose someone until well into their adult lives.

We also tend to hush and cover-up death now, and, in particular, to shield children from it. It is not usually talked about, except when it has already occurred. Even discussing an imminent death is often felt to be in poor taste, as if the event were being wished for, or somehow hastened by acknowledging it. Thus we cloud death with superstition, ignorance and excessive fear.

One of the saddest stories I have heard was of a son leaving his dying mother, in case she thought it odd that he was still there past his normal going-home time. 'I didn't want her to suspect anything, and I didn't want to frighten her,' he said. She died only a short while later, alone. He has since found it difficult to forgive himself, so that the sadness associated with the episode has been multiplied. Sadness is also increased for bereaved people when friends avoid them because they don't know how to face their grief. It is the extra suffering we impose upon ourselves and others which is unnecessary, and which, perhaps, we can learn to avoid.

To begin with, have you ever thought about your own death? This is not to suggest that anyone should constantly indulge in morbid thoughts, but simply to attend, perhaps just once, to this piece of business. Contemplating your death and others' reaction to it might throw up all manner of practical considerations to begin with. Have you made a will? If so, do the right people know that you have and where to find it? What about other important papers and keys? Funeral instructions? These can be lodged with an undertaker in advance (filed under 'not yet dead'), and again should be known about by those it will concern.

One of the consequences of thinking through the practical consequences of death might be that it enables you to ease some of the burden on those left behind. Someone whose papers are accessible and in order will help loved ones at a difficult time, and also leave a message of love behind — 'I thought about you, and wanted to sort out some of the problems for you. I know that things will be hard for you just now, and, in a small way, I wanted to make some of them easier.'

There is help to be had with these tasks. The organization Cruse has produced a booklet, *Who Wants to Think About dying?*, which deals with practical topics such as making a will, and financial considerations like life assurance, funeral costs, and pension plans. The booklet also contains a checklist to be filled in, to help family members and other people like executors to find necessary information. The booklet costs 75p from Cruse (address on page 117)[1], and every home should have one.

If in these ways we can help those left behind, and ease our own minds in the process, what about the larger issues? If you have small or dependent children, what will happen to them if you should die? Is anyone else dependent on you? What about your pets? If you die tomorrow, what will happen to them?

To be able to face and answer all these questions in advance of death is not morbid, but reassuring and useful. They should not be left vague or unattended to, for everyone's sake. We are stronger for facing our fears, not weaker. It is not always easy to contemplate one's own death, but to do so in the hope of easing the future of loved ones is surely better than brushing it aside as if it is unimportant. Think about it.

A mother of young children, dying of cancer, not only sorted out all the practical affairs she could in the last weeks of her life, but also wrote letters to her husband and children, to be opened after she had died, containing messages of love and comfort. On a different scale, an elderly man, still in good health, has distributed his extensive record collection amongst his family and friends. As he has sorted it out, he has catalogued and put on tape all the music he wants to keep. It is now lighter and easy to store, and organized so that it will not be a chore for someone to sort out after he dies. Far from being cast down by all this, it has given him (and everyone on the receiving end) much pleasure, and he feels relieved to have got it done; it was a task he wanted to complete while he was well and able to do it.

Just as keeping the practical business of life up-to-date and ready for whatever comes can be a source of relief and comfort, so can attention to more spiritual things. It is easy to think that questions about the meaning of life, the possibility of afterlife, and so on, are the concern of Higher Thinkers, but they are, or at least they should be, the concern of all of us. Our beliefs are an important part of us, and have a strong influence on behaviour and the way we react and make plans. We feel free to discuss our beliefs about politics, local, national and world-wide current events, and almost anything else that impinges on our daily lives, yet there is often a difficulty about deeper, more personal, thoughts and feelings. Perhaps thinking about death is particularly hard because it involves an element of fear of the unknown and because its inevitability threatens us all. At some time in adult life we need to bring these fears out into daylight and look at them. Reading, private thought, talking to trusted people, or attending more formal discussion groups at a church (or its equivalent) can all be useful ways of exploring the questions of life and death, alone or with your partner.

Addressing topics like this can be distressing for a while, of course, and can lead to some inner turmoil and sadness, so it is better to undertake the task with some support, and to choose the timing, if you can. Difficult things are best faced from a position of strength and optimism, so it would be better not to choose to attend to this particular kind of business when you are already feeling low. However hard the task may seem, it is important to remember that we are built for adaptation and problem-resolution, and that the aim of the exercise is a quiet mind.

Vague or half-named fears cannot be dealt with, and we tend to leave them unresolved, and so they remain just as frightening as ever. But once the fear has been named and acknowledged, it can be explored and then dealt with, and cannot then be as frightening again. By making a positive effort to deal with our fears about death, we remove the burden of it. Perhaps when we are free of that burden, we no longer need to feel distanced from others who are grieving or afraid, and who need our love and support. Someone whose mind is clear about death could explain it to a child grieving over a pet or a grandparent, for example, but what could someone still entangled with their own fears do?

Facing up to death might also enable us to talk to a dying loved one about it, and stay close to them, rather than needing to run away and leave them isolated. To remain close, and to be able to share thoughts and feelings, can ease the pain for the dying or grieving one, and can also take some of the burden of grief from the survivor. Surely not having failed someone in an hour of extreme need is a comfort? Think about that, too.

3

Different kinds of bereavement through death

No death fails to leave its mark on those closely involved, and all loss by death has a special meaning for someone. Statistical studies tell us that the loss of a parent in one's adult life is less traumatic than the loss of a spouse, and that the loss of a spouse in the young is often more traumatic than in old age. Statistics are, of course, generalizations, and they have hidden amongst them many personal stories, and many exceptions that prove rules. In discussing the prospective deaths of her parents, one woman said, 'I know I will be afraid. I'll think it'll be my turn next.' Another's response was, 'When my parents die, I know I'll be all right. I'll have to be, then. I'll have to grow up and stand on my own two feet.' The impact of loss, then, is to some extent determined by its meaning for the survivor — what does it take away? What does it leave them with? The relationship between the survivor and deceased also has a part to play, as does the quality of that relationship. How loss affects any one person will be a complex interplay of these factors. The mode of death also has an important part to play in determining the impact and outcome.

Sudden death

Death by accident or by illness of a very short duration leaves no time for us to become prepared. Shock, and extra difficulty in coming to terms with the reality of it, are often felt more strongly in these circumstances. When we can anticipate a major life-change, we can plan ahead, make arrangements, begin to adjust in advance of the event. Even though all this can seem heart-breaking, it can be reassuring. Some writers have put forward the idea of 'anticipatory grieving', which can ease the final pain of parting to some extent. Parkes[2] describes several studies which show that there is greater emotional disturbance following a death for which there was little time to prepare. We adapt better, on the whole, when we can take things one step at a time.

Disbelief when someone last seen alive and healthy, is reported as dead, is usual and can be very strong. 'How can this be? It doesn't make sense. It must be a mistake.' As reality takes hold, shock and a severe stress reaction are common. This can often be accompanied by distressing physical symptoms such as fainting, nausea, shaking, diarrhoea — the whole body is reacting to an emergency.

When the death was witnessed by someone close, for example, in a car accident, the survivor may also be overwhelmed by a sense of helplessness and personal vulnerability. 'Death has passed close by. It could have been me, or anyone, and there was nothing I could do,' is a common reaction. One's sense of personal safety and competence is suddenly snatched away.

It is not likely that anything can influence these early reactions. They represent an inevitable stress and confusional state, which will pass in the fullness of time. It *is* possible, however, for things not to be made worse than they already are, whatever the cause of death, whatever the immediate antecedents or consequences. The living must be the focus of concern now — the dead are beyond our tending. The living need quiet, respect for their grief, their needs listened to and attended to as far as possible. If they want to stay with the body for a while, that is their decision, and it is not up to anyone else to decide what is best. If they do not want to see the body, they should not be pressured to, even though it is known that to do so helps reality to be accepted. How the choice is presented is important. Undue pressure can be detrimental, but stressing that the loved one is peaceful can help to sway the decision. While gentle warning of any change or mutilation is essential, it is important to realize that the professional carer will not see the body through the eyes of close loved ones. If the body is in hospital, medical clutter needs to be removed from its immediate vicinity, but it is also important to make it known that everyone tried to do all that was possible. This should be explained in simple terms; people in shock tend to misunderstand and or misinterpret anything complex.

In hospital, or elsewhere, the question of whether the person suffered will need to be addressed. Many people will ask outright, some will not be able to, but will indicate by their questions and comments that they want to know. Sometimes, the confident, honest answer can be 'No', but when this is not the case, lying about it (even with the kindest of intentions) is likely to lead to extra pain. The bereaved will often realize that it is not true, and may be lead to imagine that it was all very much worse than it really was. It is no service to them, and it is always better to find a way of being truthful, but perhaps stressing that the pain was brief, or unconsciousness intervened — to give whatever comfort there may be. It is important that everyone involved should be consistent and should keep their explanations brief and simple, in order not to overload the capacity for understanding, which is often adversely affected in those under stress. Someone should undertake to give continuing support and to answer any further questions later if need be. Any decision which does not need immediate attention should be left until the initial shock has subsided.

Even with the best early care there is, those closely involved with sudden death tend to remain vulnerable. The Harvard study [3] showed a significant degree of emotional disturbance in young widows, which persisted throughout the first year of bereavement following the sudden death of their husbands. Other studies on close relatives unexpectedly bereaved have found long persisting poor health coupled with intense grief, guilt and depression. A particularly striking example of this was highlighted in a study carried out by Shanfield, Swain and Benjamin in 1985 [4]. The reactions of parents who had lost adult children with cancer were compared with those where the loss had been by accident. The long-term, intense grief pattern in the accident victim's parents was compared with the cancer victim's parents. Over half of the cancer victims' parents felt that they had experienced personal growth and spiritual strength, and become closer to each other.

What can we learn from this and other studies is that those who are suddenly bereaved need extra-special care in the weeks and months following the death. The positive impact of bereavement counselling, with its opportunities to talk through feelings in an uncritical atmosphere, has been demonstrated in studies mentioned earlier. Friendship and consistent support from those around can also help to offset the worst effects of sudden loss, as can gentle advice about self-care (the need for rest, good nutrition, exercise, relaxation, self-esteem building with good close friends) and pastoral and spiritual comfort. The need for more formal psychiatric or psychological help should also be recognized if grief and guilt do not seem to be resolving or if they are major, persistent preoccupations.

Suicide

For many, if not most people, death is a hard thing to come to terms with. Typically, we struggle to stay alive under the most adverse circumstances; we put enormous amounts of time, effort, skill and resources into curing the sick; we feel triumphant when someone has been snatched back from the brink of death by medical endeavour or by chance. Life is, for the most part, sweet. That someone close to us should *choose* death in preference to life overturns all the hopes and beliefs that our striving to live entails, and challenges our need to find life meaningful.

Death by suicide is usually sudden, with all the extra burden of grief and guilt it leaves behind. It will usually have been preceded by difficulties in close personal relationships and disturbed behaviour, often involving much bitterness, grief and anger, which now cannot be put right. These two factors alone are additional burdens, over and above those associated with more usual kinds of bereavement. Further, suicides are often preceded by threats or warnings which were not noticed or not taken seriously at the time, so the 'if only . . .' feeling characteristic of guilt is reinforced.

The tendency, present in all of us to a greater or lesser extent, to feel guilty when someone dies, and angry, and to look around for someone to blame or turn the blame in on the self, can only be exacerbated in suicidal death. There is also evidence from research that the surviving relatives of suicides, particularly spouses, may experience a variety of negative reactions from those around them.[5] These may range from failure to offer the usual kinds of social support to the bereaved, through withdrawal, to overt hostility. The uncomfortable challenge thrown down for us by suicide clearly has an effect on many more people than the immediate family and close friends. It is a challenge to all of us, perhaps, and one we seem ill-prepared to deal with. The anger, in particular, is generated by the action of the person who has committed suicide, who slaps us all in the face by choosing death, but since there is a taboo against being angry with the dead, it gets diverted on to the living. Perhaps also, each person touched by it wonders what their own part in that death was, by default or even by direct action. Someone once said that the message a suicide leaves behind is, 'Look at what you made me do.' Perhaps 'Look what you failed to stop me doing' is nearer the mark. In either event, suicide seems often to generate wide ripples of remorse, guilt, anger and bewilderment. Some cultures and faiths ban suicides from the usual death rites, and exclude them from burial in consecrated ground. Ghastly folk-legends abound about them. All this demonstrates the struggle we have, and perhaps have always had, to understand the person who chooses death. The exceptions seem to be those courteous and thoughtful people who, perhaps faced with terminal illness or the threat of declining powers, tidy up all their earthly business, leave letters of love and explanation behind, and plan death so as to be as little distressing to others as possible, but these are rare. It is much more common for suicide to be the culmination of a period or periods of desperate unhappiness and distress for all involved.

Then there are the legal and forensic accompaniments of suicide. Often, someone still in a state of considerable shock after the death, in no state to take things in or think clearly, will be required to answer searching questions. Perhaps they will have to face horrors like having to leave the body, which may be mutilated by the mode of death, where it is while police photographers do their work; perhaps they will be asked to identify a badly mutilated body. These things pile nightmare upon nightmare. Legal requirements tend to override any consideration for the state of the bereaved. This fact-gathering may be necessary, but it is a compelling thought that perhaps there is an element of that anger and rejection running through it all.

Paul Lodge[6] has argued for a change in procedures, to protect the living, who should, after all, be the focus of care now. There may be a need for society's institutions to establish the causes and the objective facts about the death, but it should not come before the emotional needs of those caught up in this peculiarly distressing form of bereavement. No one is truly in a position to judge what might have seemed to be a difficult relationship between the suicide and those close to them, much less to get inside the head of someone who has decided to commit suicide. We can only know that it is something outside the normal experience of most of us, and therefore not to be judged by our usual criteria. In these circumstances, we would do better to look to the needs of the living instead, and these will be the same as those of anyone newly and suddenly bereaved, the need for care and comfort, for reassurance, uncritical advice, and professional help when the usual human kindliness is not enough to prevent a pathological grief reaction.

Difficult death

Many people would opt for quietly dying while they are asleep, or very suddenly with no time to think about what was happening, if they could choose. Some might like to slip away in the arms of loved ones, all goodbyes having been said and earthly business done. Unhappily, there are deaths where none of this can be true. Death which is neither quick nor easy, and which is witnessed by close survivors, can leave an appalling legacy of grief behind. In some terminal illnesses, pain cannot be controlled, even though it is rare for that to be so; some accidents and disasters lead to painful, lingering death. Events such as these produce memories, seemingly etched into the minds of survivors with painful clarity, which are remarkably resistent to fading. Fifteen, twenty years after witnessing deaths like these, people can recount the events with great vividness, and, at the same time, produce in themselves acute distress and grieving. Nothing can undo the tragedy, but perhaps it can be prevented from becoming a multiple tragedy and ruining other lives. It needs to be let go. A first step is to realize that the bad memory is only one memory, or only one episode, or a few episodes. Does it negate *all* the others, all the happiness, all the other precious scenes which made up a life? The bad memory can sometimes be like a hair shirt, it begins as an act of penance or expiation, but eventually becomes a thing in its own right, a penance that can never be completed. It does not serve the dead to castigate the living. We serve both the dead and the living best by concentrating on the good times and the good things, so that we can allow ourselves to be happy. If that seems to be impossible without help, it should be acknowledged to be a problem, and help should be sought. The organization Cruse would be a good first contact. If further, intense work on this unresolved grief is needed, then professional assistance from a psychologist or psychiatrist will be necessary. The dead are safe and beyond our keeping, and our first priority should be the care and comfort of the living, who are still with us, and whose lives are still open to influence and healing. If this is you, or someone close to you, do think about taking the first step towards it by picking up a pen or a telephone. There are addresses and telephone numbers on pages 117-119, and your local health practitioner or clinic, or civic information centre could also be places to start. Good luck.

4

The nature of grief

Grief has often been likened to a journey — a walk in the valley of shadows, for example. If it *is* a journey, it is by no means a straight path, but a tortuously winding one, where the traveller can become bogged down, or side-tracked, or injured by hazards met along the way. Worst of all, perhaps, is to appear to be making progress, only to find oneself back at an earlier stage, or having to start all over again. This is what the journey through grief can be like. It is a journey that perhaps none of us would choose to make, and we are often pushed off on it when we feel at our least able, and at a time when we do not want to go through with it, but have no choice.

The very last thing that you would want to hear, as a reluctant, weak and battered traveller at the beginning of a difficult journey, is that, in the end, you will benefit from it. Nevertheless, unwelcome and unacceptable though that message might be, it can be true. Coming to terms with loss and grief can be a hard and bitter struggle, but it can result in personal growth, new awareness and strength.

Grief can also be seen as a series of tasks you need to accomplish. Each one must be finished before the next one can be begun. To each one you bring strengths and weaknesses from the past. The weaknesses need to be confronted and overcome, or they will hold you up, and prevent the finishing of the task. Your strengths and resources, and those of others around you, will be there to help you. Understanding the process is a necessary first step.

One of the aims of this book is to help the reader to explore the stresses involved in grief, and to try to bring some of the useful work in talking through these problems, to the written page. Often in periods of stress, calm logical thought seems impossible. The mind races or goes blank, concentration is poor. It may be that help and information, presented in a clear and simple way, in a form which can be picked up and put down, taken in so much at a time, and re-read where necessary, could be of practical use at such a time.

It is a very natural, human thing to listen, to talk together, to try to work towards resolution of some of the pain and problems associated with loss. It is very much harder to write something designed to be illuminating and helpful without the benefit of that close human contact, but it seems important to try.

First, because there is a need for information about reactions to loss, particularly some of the many complex emotions associated with it. People are so often frightened of their own 'odd' feelings and thoughts under the impact of grief — to know that these are all part of a necessary process might be helpful. Secondly, those around someone who has been bereaved often feel at a loss to know the 'right' thing to say or do, or how to help. We (the human race at large, that is) sometimes seem to be very bad at dealing with one another's grief. The accounts of recently bereaved people contain many instances of apparent rejection by others. 'People cross the road to avoid me, or pretend they haven't seen me.'

Sometimes, a grieving person just turns up on the doorstep of a friend or relative, or telephones at a moment of anguish, and may find themselves in a situation of uncomfortable silence. They know then that they and their grief are causing embarrassment. 'I didn't know what to say,' the recipient of the call may say later, conscious of having fallen short in some way, but not knowing how they could have made it better. In this way, the grieving can be under pressure to hide their feelings so that they don't upset others, and this can be another burden on them. Situations like this arise, not from unkindness, but because someone facing us with feelings we have not come to terms with ourselves can be threatening. Not facing and dealing with our own grief can make us vulnerable to someone else's. Perhaps that is why people sometimes go out of their way to avoid the bereaved. That is only one of a number of good reasons for working at one's own feelings. Such work is strengthening, and can ultimately help us to deal with others in a compassionate and unembarrassed way.

Being so afraid of death that we avoid anyone who has recently been associated with it, is another aspect of the problem. However, the time must come when that fear is faced and explored and resolved, otherwise it is not only a constant background threat to us, but it can cut us off from those who are grieving and who are in need of our help and comfort. It could remain as an undeveloped or immature part of the self, which might otherwise grow to be an integrated part of a whole adult, with all its rich capacity for caring and hoping, living and sharing through grief and joy. For people who have no direct experience of grief and mourning a first small step might be taken by reading one of the books which have recently come on the market about it. Although we cannot learn the 'right' way to grieve from a book, nor can knowledge and understanding abolish grief, what we know and accept is often less frightening than the unknown. Increasing understanding can serve to diminish fear. If some of the fear and bewilderment in the emotional complexities of grief can be reduced, confidence in the self and its ability to change, adapt and grow, might be enhanced.

5

Early grief: the impact of stress

The immediate response to sudden losses like unexpected redundancy, learning that you will never walk again, hearing that a loved one has just died, is usually a period of frozen immobility. The impact of the event is overwhelming. We call it 'shock'. The person who has received the news, or witnessed the event, may seem almost paralysed by it. They may not move at all, or may do so as if moving were unfamiliar or painful. Speech may not come easily, and it may be hard to take things in. I remember the frozen-in-time, dreamlike state when, in my childhood, someone came to say that my great-grandmother had died. The scene is captured in my mind, as if on a slow-motion film. The words hung in the air, 'I've got some bad news, I'm afraid . . .' It did not seem to make any sense.

Perhaps the 'shutdown' we experience, which can be momentary or can last some hours or even days, protects us. It is too much to take in and deal with all at once, and so we shut ourselves off for a while. We will have to attend to what has happened and be dealing with all kinds of practical details soon enough, but, in the very beginning, we pause awhile; it is a necessary part of coming to terms with our loss.

Those close to someone at this stage of grief need to remember that this is no time to hand them lots of information, or expect them to make complex decisions. They need to be peaceful and quiet, to be looked after gently, not fussed, but not left by themselves. On the other hand, they should not be left out of important decisions because they do not appear to be fully capable. Leaving someone out now might be a cause of bitter regret later. Decisions can usually wait a while, and this earliest stage soon passes.

Even when it does, however, the bereaved person will still be struggling with enormous amounts of feelings and thoughts. There is a great deal of adapting to do, and it cannot all be done at once. They may appear simple and concrete in their thinking or less than rational, but it is all quite understandable in view of what they are dealing with inside themselves. It is fortunate, in a way, that our society imposes certain formalities when someone dies because dealing with them may be a first step on the path to taking in full reality. We may not be thinking at our best, but, after the initial shock phase, we can fill in forms and perhaps choose, or help to choose, things like hymns and flowers for the funeral. Anyone newly bereaved should be encouraged, if need be, to be involved in these decisions. We need to protect them still, but we must avoid over-protecting them. If someone has strong views — like seeing the deceased one's body, or *not* seeing it — those wishes should be respected. No one should take it upon themselves to decide that someone else 'isn't up to it' or 'it might upset them'. Yes, it might, but that is a real and important upset, and all part of the grieving process. We should not try to prevent someone expressing grief, nor should we be afraid if the emotion is intense. It is better not bottled up. Someone in the initial stages of grief is vulnerable, and we need to listen to their needs and respect their wishes; to share the burden, but not to take it from them.

These early turbulent feelings are often difficult to cope with, and it seems particularly hard that they should be so strong at such a painful time. They are part of the 'fight or flight' mechanism we all possess, the function of which is to get us out of danger, and they represent the body's attempt to deal with a situation perceived as dangerous and threatening. When the danger is a physical threat like a predatory animal, the mechanism serves us well, but when it is a crisis we can neither fight nor run from, this mechanism can cause a period of emotional and physical upheaval. In a situation such as a major loss, which we cannot escape from by running away, the body is all charged up for action but the extra energy has nowhere to go, and it produces a range of uncomfortable physical sensations like the heart pounding and strange feelings or even pain in the chest. This is because extra oxygen would be needed by the muscles in a 'flight' situation, so the heart and lungs are working extra hard. Blood will be diverted to the muscles from deep organs like the gut, so that in a period of intense stress, the gut does not function properly. Digestive disorders of various kinds, like nausea and diarrhoea are therefore common.

Any living creature under threat needs to be extra alert, so sleep is often badly disturbed, and everything seems to impinge on the senses with increased force during the waking day. In addition, there are feelings of intense anxiety or fear in the early stages of grief after loss.

Suddenly, the world has an unfamiliar quality, which feels dangerous. The panic of a child who looks around and realizes that it is in a strange place, or suddenly cannot see its mother, is the same kind of feeling. Perhaps you have felt it before, when something strange presented itself in a familiar setting, or when something which had always been there in its usual place, was unaccountably missing. There is a quickening of the heart, and a rush of fear. We depend on the world having stable elements in it, things we can predict with certainty, for our sense of security. To be bereaved is to lose an important one of those elements, so it is not surprising that we should react by feeling unsafe and threatened. The opening of C.S. Lewis' helpful book, *A Grief Observed*[7] is a comment on how grief feels like fear, and he describes the sensations, which are like those when one is afraid. These feelings of fear may come and go, or may remain a fairly constant background feature for some time. Often, when they seem to have subsided, they return from time to time. They may be triggered by a certain event or memory, or by excessive tiredness, or they may come for no clear reason.

However, as the new situation after loss becomes familiar with the passage of time and a new set of predictable events evolve, these feelings of fear and disorientation subside. The speed and ease with which a more settled state is achieved will depend on a number of things:

● *Was there time to prepare?* Research into transitions like redundancy and retirement and the death of a loved one, all show that time to adapt in advance of the event tends to lead to a better outcome

● *How big is the change?* How many different aspects of life will be affected? If the loss of a job or a loved one or a limb, also involves moving house, and a changed financial position, these are extra stresses on top of the primary source of stress, and can cause additional problems

● *Who is around to help?* The presence of caring, steadfast friends and relatives can make all the difference to the outcome

● *What was life like before the loss?* If there was a difficult, unhappy relationship with the loved one or with the work situation, the outcome will be adversely affected. It seems less destructive to lose something good than to lose something emotionally complicated, with a lot of 'unfinished business' attached to it

● *What about the inner state of the bereaved?* An anxious, clinging person, or someone already in poor physical or mental health will have a hard time achieving a good outcome.

All these things are pointers to how a person may react to bereavement. They highlight possible danger areas, where extra input of care and resources might be needed.

During the early days after loss has been experienced when the shock and the acute stress reaction have begun to ease, many other emotions crowd in. There are often feelings of restlessness and yearning. Something precious is lost, and a deep instinct tells us to move around, search until we find it and restore it to its rightful place. The rational part of the brain knows that we cannot do it, but a more instinctive part of us is moved to try. The split between logic and longing is often very painful and difficult to deal with. It may be something never experienced before. As time passes, however, it eases. When the pain of longing is acute, it is sometimes helpful to have something to hold or carry around which is closely associated with the lost one. One widow took her husband's old dressing-gown to bed to hold in her arms. She missed him badly at night, and the bed seemed too big without him, but the feel of the old familiar garment made it easier for her. She held it almost instinctively, and sometimes we do need to trust to our instincts, and others around should allow these things to happen without critical comments or advice to stop.

Other people may prefer to deal with the restlessness by walking a great deal, or turning out the kitchen, or some other form of absorbing physical activity. That is not odd either — it is simply a response to a distress so deeply upsetting that it demands activity. The cause of it cannot be dealt with directly yet, so the needs it produces must be channelled into something else for the moment.

Helplessness

When ordinary things go wrong, most people react by bustling about until they are put right again. We are used to the idea that we can sort things out with time and effort and will, or that, if we cannot, we can contact someone who can. An irreversible loss such as bereavement might be the first thing someone encounters that they cannot put right, no matter how hard they try, even with all the skills, talents and resources at their disposal, and no matter how much they long to make it all right again. This is hard to face, and it is not surprising that it often produces feelings of helplessness.

I can remember thinking at the funeral of a friend how much we all had wanted her to live. I looked around at a church full of strong, capable people. So many of us, all used to feeling that we were in control of things, and not a thing that any or all of us could do had kept her alive. No wonder that we feel helpless in the face of death, and that it takes a while to shake that feeling off. Like the fear, helplessness is a natural part of the reaction to loss. Like the fear, it will pass with time and work. None of the people at that funeral could keep our friend alive, but we could comfort and sustain the family, see that the children got to and from school, provide hot meals. In carrying out small but useful tasks, we fight off helplessness and give each other time to recover.

Anger

To use the comparison of a lost child and the feelings of early grief, often the child's reaction on being united with its parent is a burst of anger. 'You lost me!' Sometimes the parent feels it too, and does not know whether to hug or smack the child. We are angry when someone deserts us. If it is someone who has walked out or gone off with someone else, perhaps, or gone because they no longer want us — we feel angry and resentful as well as sad, as we do when the employer says, 'We don't want you any more.' But can we feel angry with someone who has left us by dying? Yes, we can, and we do. Again, logic is defeated by strong emotion. We may feel deserted, rejected even, and left to face the world alone, so anger is a natural response, even though logic may tell us that there is no one to blame.

This is such a difficult dilemma that anger frequently gets displaced on to someone else. A classic example was the only son of a very elderly mother. They had always lived together, and were very close. When she died at age 93 of a rare and inoperable cancer, his response was, 'If the doctors had done more, they could have saved her!' Perhaps he was really saying, 'How could she go, and leave me on my own?'

When we are angry, we tend to look for someone to blame. Sometimes with more or less justice, we fix on another person. Sometimes, the anger is turned in on oneself. 'I shouldn't have . . .', 'If only I had . . .', 'I wish I'd been . . .'. It can also be the first real challenge to faith. A lifelong churchgoer recently said after being left on his own, 'There can't be a God; He wouldn't let these things happen.' To feel the anger at a time like this is natural and understandable, but we need to guard against it becoming self-destructive, an anger which cuts us off from earthly or spiritual sources of help and comfort, because it can then go on generating itself, and turn to bitterness. This is when it needs talking through with a counsellor or trusted friend, taken out and looked at in daylight, as it were. Then, the feeling can be explored and experienced free of the tangle of blame and guilt, and it can begin to be resolved.

Nothingness

While the predominant feeling of early grief is sadness, often mixed with fear and anger, there are also sometimes episodes of a strange absence of emotion — flatness, nothingness, as if one had gone beyond all feeling. It is likely that these represent an overloaded system 'switching off'. In early grief, so much strong emotion is felt in a relatively short space of time that, every now and then, the need to shut down for a while seems to take over. These automaton-like times may worry those around the bereaved person, but they are probably as necessary as sleep. During these episodes, there can be a feeling of detachment from the world and everyone in it. 'What has this got to do with me?' Grief and joy in others are equally meaningless, nothing touches or impinges on the bereaved person. Sometimes, even the speech of others makes no sense; not enough effort can be put into listening to someone talking to give it meaning. This is no time, however, to leave someone alone. They may not be easy to be with, but in spite of appearances, will need the company of caring and undemanding others, who will need to be patient and to accept apparent rebuffs until the mood passes.

Positive feelings

It may seem strange that in the midst of grief, feelings of happiness can take over. Many recently bereaved people have described experiences in which, often unaccountably, heaviness of heart is eased. A sense of joy or peace takes the place of sorrow. Sometimes, the heightened awareness that accompanies fear and anxiety, shades over into elation. There may be a feeling of joyful expectancy. It is almost as if the loss is not real, and at any moment the loved one will reappear, and everyone will laugh with relief, and say, 'What a silly mistake we made.' Sometimes, a strong sense of the presence of the loved one accompanies the new feeling. These are precious moments in the midst of acute grief, and they give much needed respite.

Sometimes the feeling is one of deep peace, which brings with it the certainty that all is well with the loved one. At such times, it is tempting to believe that grieving is over and done. Unfortunately, like the feeling of joy or elation, these episodes are usually brief, and tend to vanish as suddenly and unaccountably as they came. However, they are times of much-needed relief, and they also bring a foretaste of the peace of mind that will come one day. C.S. Lewis describes how, quite unexpectedly one morning, his heart felt lighter. He had slept better than he usually did the night before, and the sun was shining when he woke. At the moment when he seemed less grief-stricken than he had before, he could suddenly remember his wife most clearly. It was as if sorrow had been a barrier between himself and his dead wife, and it had lifted. This was not the end of grief — it happened in the early weeks after her death — but it was the real beginning of hope for him.

Denial

I dislike the term 'denial' — it sounds as if the person described as doing it is being stubborn or awkward somehow, or at least, as if it were a conscious thing. By denial, we mean a range of thoughts, beliefs, perceptions, feelings, which are concerned with the continued existence and presence of the dead. For example, the belief that the report of the death is a mistake, and that someone coming to the door will have a message to prove it. A client described vividly his conviction that a woman standing in the street was a social worker who had come from the hospital to say that his wife had not died after all, it was a mistake. In fact, she was simply a woman waiting for a bus. His hope was so strong that it had taken on its own reality — until the bus came. These events are much more likely when the bereaved person is not present when the loved one dies, and can be very powerful indeed when the body has not been seen, or there is no body. A woman whose son had been lost at sea had these episodes for years afterwards, as hope refused to die. Sometimes we 'see' the person who has died. I 'saw' a friend who had recently died dozens of times in familiar places. She lived close by, we used the same shops, our children went to school together. In life I met her very often. After she died, it only needed a slightly similar hairstyle or coat on someone and I was ready to say 'Hello' — but in the very same instant, I knew it could not be her. A friend who had recently lost her son said that she sometimes found herself following young men. Something about the clothes or general physique startled her into noticing, and the strong need of her dead son took over a while. She never approached them or spoke to them, of course. She knew with one part of her what the rest of her that longed for him so much could not yet take in.

Sometimes this struggle to adjust takes the form of vivid dreams about the dead person, in which they are still alive. These dreams have a quality of reality about them which is so strong and comforting that waking from them is a shock. Liz McNeil Taylor reports such dreams in her book, *Living with Loss*.[8] The brief joy and respite granted in sleep seems cruel, as waking to reality snatches it away.

What are we to make of this? First, the habit of being with, and seeing that person, often for years and years, is a very strong influence. We are tuned in to their presence; it may be part of our daily expectation. We can hardly switch it off in a moment when so many other familiar things remain around us. It takes time to adjust. Also, we are in a heightened state of awareness in the weeks after someone has died, because it is a new situation, and we are always alert in new situations. This very alertness makes it more likely that we will jump to conclusions about similar-looking clothes and other such things. Then there is our need to make order of chaos, to lean towards the familiar, and to interpret things around us as fitting into categories we are used to. All these things tend to make us interpret events in certain ways.

There is also, and perhaps more importantly, our longing for the loved one. This can be so strong that it overcomes logic and reason. Perhaps in bereavement, it is the first time that you have come across the complexities in your nature, or been aware that the logical, intelligent brain on which we tend to rely so heavily, is only one part of our mind's functioning. It lives side by side with deeper, more instinctive parts of the self, and sometimes in extreme need, they are the stronger. Nothing is lost by facing these truths about ourselves; indeed in the end they can be enriching.

In the days that follow a bereavement, all these thoughts and feelings tend to be strong, to dominate one's life, and to change rapidly from minute to minute. A mood can change from black despair to deep peace and relief, to anger, to tears, often for no obvious reason, and without warning. The body's natural rhythms are also often disturbed; sleepless nights are common, as is dropping briefly into sleep during the day. Appetite may vary between bursts of hunger, and episodes of nausea, or the feeling of not being able to swallow. Distressing symptoms like palpitations or chest pains may occur. Frequency of urine and tummy upsets can also happen, and people report feeling dizzy, lightheaded, off-balance. Tennyson describes this as being 'drunk with loss'.

All these things are part of the upheaval following a major shock, as we struggle to take in and cope with too many changes all at once. It is rather like struggling through a violent storm, being battered from all sides whilst desperately trying to stay on course and keep on your feet.

In a real storm, a good strategy would be to plod on patiently, seeking rest and shelter wherever possible, looking after one's physical needs, and hanging on until it passes. The best kind of companion would be one who stayed the course and made no demands, who eased the burden just by being there, and was sensitive to needs as they arose. So it is in early grief. No one needs chiding, advising, being told what they should be doing, thinking or feeling. The need is to be allowed to feel and express whatever comes, whether that means crying for hours, talking until the small hours and sleeping until noon, walking in the rain — and for those around to accept it all, and still be there beside you, holding on.

Susan Hill has written an excellent and moving account of the first year of bereavement in her book, *In the Springtime of the Year.*[9] It is a novel, but contains a great deal of the truth of early grief. She describes how, in the first weeks, Ruth, a young widow, had gone up and down the stairs, stood in the middle of one room or another, talking to herself or to her dead husband, often in a dreamlike state. Sometimes she felt as if nothing had changed, but at the same time she knew the truth with another part of her mind. She could not sleep in the bed they had shared, so cat-napped in a chair; could not face cooking, nor eating properly, was restless and distracted. No one helped or was able to help her except Jo, her dead husband's young brother, who came quietly to help with chores and keep her company, and to stay by her in a calm, compassionate way while she struggled through her grief. He offered practical help when she was exhausted, but was sensitive enough not to do too much for her, and so take over her life. He kept on coming, quietly and undemandingly, no matter how he found her, until she began to come through the dark days. In the book, Jo is a teenager, but he is possessed of a mature wisdom which enables him to stay the course with Ruth. He is the best kind of companion.

6

What is helpful?

The intensity of the pain in the early days of grief inevitably lessens with time, but for most people it is not a smooth fading away. The shock of acute grief gives way to periods of some relief, interspersed with episodes of pain and longing, fear, anger, guilt and all the other thoughts and feelings which dominated life at the onset. These episodes take their toll during the weeks and months following bereavement, and a chronic feeling of tiredness is therefore quite common. Apathy, lack of interest in others, and poor concentration are also frequently seen in this stage of grief. Thoughts often turn to the death, and there may also be a painful paradoxical state in which fear of dying, and longing for death to join the loved one are intertwined. Appetite and sleep are probably still disturbed, so that people feel physically unwell and may tend to dwell on their health, and to visit the doctor more often than usual.

In this stage, people around sometimes find it hard to cope and may withdraw or become irritated, or hint that one should be 'getting over it' or 'getting on with life'. Such reactions can serve to increase the sense of isolation and loss in the bereaved person. There is no 'should' about it. The healing process, the adaptation, takes its own time and cannot be speeded up at will. It is going on, even through times which might appear to be mere repetitions of earlier feelings. It is no help to be told, 'Don't think about it, it will only upset you; don't talk about it, it won't bring them back.' There is great value in being allowed to express thoughts and feelings, even if they are distressing or appear pointless to an outsider. The listener needs to suspend judgement, and simply to be an all-accepting ear. So often we feel compelled to say *something*, and so often we get it wrong. In 1984 a research team in America interviewed 25 people who had experienced a death in their immediate family.[10] They asked about the kind of responses they received from people who knew about the bereavement and if they were helpful or unhelpful. Eighty per cent of responses were felt to be unhelpful. Among the kinds of comments felt to be unhelpful were the following:

> He (God) had a purpose
> It's God's will
> Be thankful you have another son
> I know how you feel
> Time makes it easier
> You shouldn't question God's will
> You have to keep on going
> You have to get on with your life
> It's inevitable
> You're not the only one who suffers
> That's over now, let's not dwell on it
> The living must go on
> She has led a full life.

Clearly, these are kindly meant, but somehow they missed the mark with the bereaved people, who did not want to be told what they should be feeling or thinking.

In contrast, comments felt to be helpful tended to be supportive, understanding, sharing, as follows:

> Come and be with us now
> You're being very strong
> It's okay to be angry at God
> It must be hard to accept
> That must be painful for you
> You must have been very close to him
> Tell me how you're feeling
> How can I be of help?
> Let's spend some time together
> Go ahead and grieve
> People really cared for him
> I'm praying for you.

These comments do not instruct or admonish, they give a message that says, 'I'm with you and feeling for you.' It may not seem like much, but it is likely to mean a lot more than any advice. Often it can be a wordless message.

Where the bereaved person lacks this kind of support, because of a depleted family or social circle, or because friends and relatives are at a loss to know how to deal with the grief, there are other possible sources of help. Cruse has trained bereavement counsellors who can be of great help through difficult times, and the hospice movement which is a growing force in the care of the dying and the bereaved also has an expanding counselling service. Patient, uncritical assistance through this time can make a real contribution to a good outcome. In 1977, Beverley Raphael, working in Australia, identified a group of widows who were particularly at risk following their husbands' deaths.[11] Risk factors were things like a non-supportive social network, traumatic circumstances of the death, an ambivalent marital relationship, and the presence of a concurrent life-crisis (such as illness). The at-risk widows were randomly assigned either to receive support for their grief and encouragement of mourning, or to receive no intervention. They were followed up at 13 months, and their general health was investigated. There was a significant lowering of ill-health in the supported group. In the non-intervention group there was a high frequency of symptoms such as sleeplessness, back pain, rheumatism, poor appetite, swollen and painful joints, feelings of panic and excessive sweating, excessive tiredness, weight loss, more visits to the doctor, increased smoking, drinking, tablet-taking, depression, and decreased work capacity.

The giving of support and counselling after bereavement is not costly, nor is it complicated, and it has a clear impact on subsequent health. The results have been repeated in other countries by other researchers, notably by Parkes in 1981.[12] He identified the surviving spouses of 181 people who had died, and at 20 months after the bereavement they were given a questionnaire which identified a potential poor-outcome group. The questionnaire looked at such things as length of time of preparation for death (from fully prepared to totally unprepared), clinging and pining (never, to constant and intense) anger (normal to extreme, bitter) self-reproach (none, to extreme) family (warm and supportive to not supportive or no family) and coping (well to very badly). All those identified as possible poor-outcome cases were assigned either to a non-intervention group, or to a group receiving bereavement support from a counsellor. Comparison of the supported and unsupported groups showed that support reduced the risk of poor outcome. In particular, the consumption of drugs, alcohol and tobacco was reduced, as were symptoms of anxiety and tension. In addition, the support service may also reduce the need for doctors and hospitals, and improve the overall level of content-ment. Dr. Parkes concludes that a bereavement support service can be shown to be effective, humane and economical.

It seems little enough to offer those in need, particularly when its effects can be so dramatically helpful.

Even with the best of help, however, some degree of depression will follow as part of the process of adapting to loss. Several factors will help to determine the degree to which depression will be experienced by the bereaved; some are described in the following chapter.

7

Depression

Like so many words used to describe personal feelings, depression tends to be vague and general. We all know roughly what it means, but it cannot tell us about another person's state in any meaningful way all by itself.

When someone says, 'I'm depressed', they can mean anything from feeling a little bit low, through a heavy persistent feeling of sadness, to a severe and prolonged disturbance of mind and body which amounts to illness. Almost any pleasant distraction might lift a lowered mood, but nothing short of the appropriate medical treatment will influence the illness. The depression which often follows bereavement can arise in many different degrees of severity, and a number of different factors will influence it. For example, if the bereaved person has always been a rather sensitive person with a tendency to episodes of depression, it might be expected that they will be badly affected by loss. Who we have lost, and what difference it will make to our lives, is another factor. The death of a spouse or a child under twenty seems to have more effect on the subsequent mental health of the survivors than does the death of parents in adult life, or the deaths of other more remote relatives. Sometimes loving relationships can become too close, becoming channels for all affectionate feelings, and perhaps taking up most of the time. Losses like these can leave too large a hole in the survivor's life, and depression may follow.

Strange though it may seem, the loss of someone close to us, about whom we have had strong but negative feelings, can also lead to a period of difficult grief and perhaps depression. While life goes on, there is always the chance of righting wrongs or resolving bad feelings or quarrels. When death robs us of that chance, the burden of all that was wrong can remain, and sometimes grow and become unbearable.

How someone has died is also an important determinant of the future problems of those left behind. A peaceful death, with time to say goodbye, and with life's work well done, is perhaps the ideal, but of course it does not always happen like that. When death comes as a kindly release and rest for worn-out bodies and minds, we can feel thankful for it. When it is an untimely snatcher of the young, taking our hopes and dreams away, or when it is the end of a horrible or painful illness or accident, the impact is very different. Sometimes such a death is witnessed by the survivors who then have those dreadful memories with them for ever. Sometimes, the survivor may be implicated in the death — a moment's inattention to a young child can, on occasion, be fatal. The awful heavy burden of guilt must then also be carried. Death by suicide can also leave an extra burden behind it.

Finally, the way in which people manage this stage of grief will also be influenced by their personal and social circumstances. Are they alone now? Are they financially worse off now? Will they have to move house? Are they young and fit, with lots of capacity to adapt, or are they old, ill or disabled? Are they well supported by family, friends, religious or other groups or not? Are they working or not?

It can be seen from all these factors that we can, in some degree, predict those people who might be at risk of sinking into the kind of depression which will need extra, perhaps medical, help. Prediction will also allow some of the risk factors to be mitigated. Extra care and support for those at risk, counselling, assistance with burdensome practical details, acknowledgement of the need to mourn, encouragement to maintain self-care (rest, nutrition, and so on) — all these things can help to protect the vulnerable, and may prevent the depression becoming a real illness.

The nature of depression

People who are depressed may cry a lot, or only occasionally. They may feel sad, or go beyond any feeling to a grey emotional flatness. Depression can feel rather like being in a glass box, able to see all that is going on around you, but yet be cut off from it.

When feelings do emerge, they may not be the expected kind, like sadness or pining, but can often be irritation and anger. A young widow remembers glaring balefully at old people in the street, and feeling furious that they were still on the earth when her husband was not.

In her moving account of the death of her baby at birth, *Nobody Told Me*,[13] Christine Simpson describes gusts of anger afterwards — wanting to throw bricks through baby-shop windows, feeling furious with mothers pushing prams, and finally venting her feelings by breaking up the room she had so lovingly prepared for her child. Between these bouts of strong emotion she was zombie-like, vague and forgetful, and wondered if she was going mad. In the end she was helped to grieve by a photograph of the baby she had never seen, and she emerged from the depression.

Not surprisingly, this stage of grief, with its difficult moods, can be the cause of great tension in families. It is the time when people need to ask unanswerable questions like, 'Why?', and the search for answers can lead to self-blame, or blaming each other. It is a time when the happiness of others can seem like an affront, and a time when the theme, 'If only . . .' goes round and round in the mind. It is a time when even an act of kindness on someone else's part can bring resentment, because it adds the burden of being grateful, when that in itself is an extra effort.

This suffering is hard, but it is a necessary part of letting go of those aspects of the old life which have gone and coming to terms with an insistent reality which will *not* go away. These things are not easily accomplished, and the disturbances of mood and thought should be seen as part of that struggle. They do not need treatment unless they shade into illness, they simply need steadfast undemanding care.

Depression as an illness

While some disturbance of sleep and appetite is to be expected after any major trauma, the passage of some days usually sees it beginning to fade. Sleep will be disturbed if the emotions are upset, and if the bereavement has changed an old habit of sleep. Sleeping in the same bed with someone, for example, can be a well-worn habit, and one which will cause disturbance if the other person is not there any more. If the loss was preceded by a time of sickness, so that those in the house were keeping half an ear open all night, or perhaps sleeping in shifts to give 24-hour care, it will take time to re-establish normal sleep patterns.

There is cause for concern when days and days go by and the normal pattern does not come back. Long hours may be spent awake, with sleep coming briefly well after midnight. Perhaps sleep comes at the right time, but lasts only a short while, and the sufferer is awake from the small hours. A disturbance of a few nights, or an odd night here and there can happen to anyone, but if a disturbed pattern becomes an established habit, it is a danger sign.

Similarly with appetite. Of course initially, when one is upset, food may feel like the last thing to be thought of, and can produce feelings of choking or nausea. However, in the normal run of events, appetite returns as emotional shock subsides. It is a cause for concern when this does not happen, even when acute distress is no longer there. Occasionally, the reverse happens, and a depressed person eats excessively.

It is also common for energy levels to be low for a while after a shock, as the body is in a 'rest and recovery' period. Self-care may be an effort. However, very low energy levels resulting in a real neglect of hygiene, failure to bother to prepare meals or tidy up or shop, and to continue in this way even when the house is in chaos and the essentials have not been bought, is a significant problem. Again, occasionally the reverse pattern is seen, and there is excessive cleaning, to the point of exhaustion.

All these things should be regarded as signs of clinical depression when they represent a significant change in normal behaviour, which does not improve even when the initial shock is over, and which are not helped at all by kindly support and counselling. They are unlikely to go away spontaneously, and will need help with medicine, or sometimes hospital treatment. There may be only one episode, the symptoms never returning, or a series of episodes with remission in between. No one should be afraid to seek help for themselves or someone else if clinical depression is suspected. Given appropriate treatment, depression usually has an excellent prognosis, and it is a common enough problem that any family doctor should be able to recognize. The best kind of treatment may involve a period of drug use, but will also use psychotherapeutic techniques designed to enhance confidence, build self-esteem, and assist planning for the future. Sometimes grief work is also carried out, if the therapist feels that mourning has not been accomplished, and help is needed to work through the process. Roughly one in three people who have suffered a major bereavement will experience some extra problems like depression, for which they will need special help.

Physical health during this stage

Anyone who has been through an intense shock, which bereavement almost always is, goes through a time of low energy and interest afterwards, as a normal part of the rest and recovery process. Even if the death was peaceful, and prepared for, it may result in several major life changes. These changes, or transitions, particularly when they involve loss, have been identified as major producers of stress. There is a growing body of evidence to suggest that such stress has implications for physical as well as mental health. For example, in the recovery period following an acute episode of stress, some of the body's immune system functions are depressed. This can lead to an increased susceptibility to infections of various kinds. In addition, since part of the immune system is implicated in certain forms of arthritis and related diseases and some types of cancer, these conditions can worsen after a period of stress. There is also a relationship between certain types of bereavement and heart disease in close survivors, particularly men after the death of a wife, and more generally among close family members following a sudden, unexpected death. At the other end of the scale of seriousness, it is usual for close family members to consult their general practitioner at an increased rate during the first year of bereavement, for a variety of causes. Bereavement can affect the health of survivors across a spectrum from minor illnesses to major or even fatal complaints.

In some societies, including our own in former years, custom demands a period of quiet and rest for mourners. Neighbours brought in food and attended to household tasks, the bereaved were not expected to exert themselves, and for a while were treated almost like invalids. There is wisdom in this approach when it aids the recovery process after shock.

Any shock, or episode of severe stress, is accompanied by rapid and dramatic changes in the body's chemistry. The body behaves as if this were in a life-threatening situation, and an arousal mechanism comes into play, to prepare the body for an intense period of physical activity. This is the so-called 'fight or flight' syndrome mentioned earlier. When the mechanism is triggered, among other things adrenalin is poured into the bloodstream, and a series of wide-ranging body changes take place. Clearly dramatic changes like these can have a bad effect when there is a pre-existing problem such as heart or artery disease, and then, in the following rest and recovery period, the immune system is also compromised for a while. Sleeplessness, poor appetite and self-neglect in the bereaved can further affect health.

Just as the likelihood of depression after loss is determined by a number of factors, so the physical health of the survivors depends on several things. Anything which increases the trauma, such as sudden, unexpected or horrific death, will increase the risks, as will pre-existing ill-heath in the survivors.

The amount of caring support available is, as always, crucial, as is the relationship between the deceased and those left. The death of a spouse seems to be particularly implicated in later health problems of the surviving partner.

Mitigating the effects

Although tranquillizers are not a good long-term method of treatment for stress, they can sometimes have their place in managing short-term crisis, particularly where the physical upheaval of stress remains a problem. Certain types called beta-blockers may also be helpful in existing heart conditions. In the medium-to-long term, however, the best help for health after a period of stress is a sound management regime.

Rest and recovery can be enhanced by the use of a regular relaxation technique, and it has been demonstrated in several studies that such techniques can have a long-term stabilizing effect on blood pressure and can reduce the risk of heart attack in coronary-prone individuals. The type of technique used is not important so long as it produces muscular relaxation and a quiet mind, and is carried out regularly (once or twice a day for at least a quarter of an hour, for about six weeks initially, and then as preferred). Yoga, Transcendental Meditation (TM) relaxation classes, autogenic hypnosis, Tai Chi, all can be excellent relaxers. There is a list of useful addresses, and further information, in *Relaxation: Modern techniques for stress management.*[14]

Nutrition is also important. It is good sense to keep to a low-fat (especially animal fat), low-salt, low-sugar, high-fibre diet, with plenty of fresh fruit and vegetables, and to keep to a varied menu. If energy is low, raw fruit needs no preparation or fuss.

Alcohol raises blood pressure, and should be avoided or used moderately.

Exercise is also beneficial, and should not be an awful chore. A brisk walk, a swim, a game of golf — all these can be pleasurable and helpful for health.

If smoking is a problem, immediately after a bereavement may not be the time to do anything dramatic about it. Everyone knows about the effect of tobacco on health. If you want to cut down, your doctor should be able to help, or to refer you on to a smoking clinic or a psychologist.

All these things — relaxation, exercise, good food, are positively helpful in maintaining health. Nurturing the spirit is equally important. Friendship, leisure activities, social groups, all these help to give a sense of well-being and fulfilment. Health is not just about the body, but about the whole person. When we ask, 'Who am I?' we do not simply count our arms and legs, but are concerned with things like our personal needs, our skills and attributes, faith, friendships, social and family roles. After the shock of bereavement, all these things need nurturing and caring for, so that we can be whole again. This middle stage of grief contains many pitfalls for our physical and mental health, but the effects can be minimized by proper self-care and the support of those around.

8

The funeral

In most human societies, and as far back as there is evidence for it, the dead have been disposed of with ritual and with reverence. Although a dead body is described in terms such as 'dust' and 'remains' and will soon decay, it once housed the essence of a beloved person, and its disposal is an opportunity to express respect, affection and sorrow. The grief of those close to the deceased is acknowledged by others, who come to support them and grieve with them. The private sorrow becomes, to some extent, public, so that the immediate society can express its involvement. By honouring the dead, we also serve the living, letting them know that their loss is felt and regretted by others. In times past, the corpse would be 'followed' by many people known to the family, who were saying in effect, 'We are with you.' The more someone was regarded with respect and affection during life, the more followers the coffin would have. They were not just following 'dust' or 'remains'.

Some years ago, two women were walking by a funeral parlour just as a hearse was coming out. Inside it was a very elaborate coffin, covered in purple fabric and with gilt handles. 'I'm appalled by the extravagance of that,' said one. 'Never mind what it must have cost. It seems unnecessary.' The other one agreed, and they went on to wonder why bodies could not be buried very simply, perhaps under the vegetable patch, or be donated to science, or be made use of in some way. 'I would not mind for myself,' said one of the women, 'but if it was my husband I would feel differently. After all, his body is a part of what I have loved all these years. I would like it to be properly and reverently laid to rest.' After a pause she added, 'And I think he would want the same for me.'

Funeral rites vary widely from society to society, and through time. They depend partly on beliefs about such things as the existence and nature of an after-life, the existence of a soul and what happens to it after death. In many cases, notably in ancient China and Egypt, bodies were buried with many possessions which they would need in after-life. In ancient Greece, bodies were buried with a coin to pay the ferryman who took the soul across a river of forgetfulness. Some funeral rites involve driving away evil spirits, or invoking the aid of good ones. Some are directed at ensuring that the spirit of the departed goes away, and does not remain on earth to 'haunt' people or places. The mystery and fear often associated with death are expressed in these ways, as is the hope that the soul will reach somewhere peaceful, beyond this life.

Funerals, then, are so much more than a farewell and the hygienic disposal of the body. They often seem to invoke grief in a very deliberate way, and involve the permanent removal from sight of the body. This final removal is a crucial part of the acceptance of the death. It is not the final letting-go, which will take some time, but it is one more step towards it; one more bond being freed.

The release of emotion is another important part of the acceptance of the death. Up until the funeral, people close to the deceased may still be in a 'frozen' state of shock, and may have difficulty in coming to terms with their loss — things may not 'sink in'. The message of the funeral rite is for some the beginning of reality. It is also often the beginning of the pain of grief. This is a necessary message, no one can readily accept, or hope to come to terms with something if its reality is in doubt. The prolonged grieving and hoping of those denied that step because the body has not been found or recovered is ample evidence of this. Bereaved people have been known to hang on to false hope for years, unable to progress through the grieving process, because no goodbye has been said, no acknowledgement of death has been made. Cases where the funeral has been unduly delayed, usually for legal reasons involving the technicalities of inquests, also take their toll of anguish from loved ones, who feel that they cannot grieve until the funeral is over. It is a significant rite of passage for those left behind.

In our society, the formal ritual of the funeral takes place a few days after someone dies, in the normal course of events. It is a time for family and friends to come together in an act of mourning and leave-taking, and it is often also a time of thanksgiving for the life of the deceased. As a ceremony which should incorporate all these many things, the modern funeral often falls a long way short. It is swift and efficient, but can leave the mourners feeling empty and cheated if it is not carried out with sufficient care.

Perhaps in an ideal world, the funeral would take place when the principal mourners felt that it was time, and not before. They would have a large say in the form the rite should take, and their wishes would be respected in all things, as far as practicable. Their right to say goodbye in their own way would be of the utmost importance. Perhaps it could be more like that even now.

There was a time when funerals were significant occasions, conducted with pomp and ritual. Everyone would know when someone in the neighbourhood had died, as blinds would be pulled down in the house, and a wreath with black ribbons placed on the door. This public statement put the onus on friends and neighbours to call and pay their respects, and also warned passers-by that quietness and reverence was expected. The bereaved wore black clothes or black armbands, so that it was immediately obvious that they were in a special state, deserving of extra thoughtfulness. The funeral procession went at walking pace, and everyone it passed would pause to acknowledge the passing of a soul, and from respect to the mourners. Those closest to the deceased would be expected to have a period of social withdrawal, and were treated with special care, almost like that given to invalids for a while. They would probably have bidden the corpse farewell with a kiss.

Nowadays, we might tend to think of all that as morbid or excessive. Perhaps it was. Although it allowed grief to be expressed, it often went further, and demanded a prolonged and extravagant period of mourning. This must often have prevented people from getting on with their lives when they felt ready to, and prevented them from letting go of the past and becoming fully reconciled to their loss and their new life. C.S. Lewis was of the opinion that, when we mourn like this, we keep the dead dead. When we let go of grief and learn to live again, we can feel closer to the loved ones we have lost than we could when overwhelmed by grief.

If our forebears over-emphasized the rituals of death and mourning, we might have gone too far the other way, and made it hard for people to express grief. We behave as though death is a source of social embarrassment, to be hushed up and put aside with as little fuss as possible. This approach is utilitarian, and can often also lead to hurried and impersonal rites. We are social beings, and have a need to express and to share our celebrations and our griefs. We need to be allowed to mourn, and to feel grief is right and natural, not something to be hidden and suppressed. Grief is, after all, an expression of love, and the funeral rites can be part of a statement about that love. No one should be pushed or rushed into having the kind of funeral for a loved one that seems inappropriate. You, the principal mourner or mourners, do not have to have a ceremony at all if you do not want to, but if you do, the form of it should be your choice, or the choice of the one who has died and left instructions.

If you should have the job of planning a funeral, take time to decide on what you want. Anyone needing a decision from you can call again, or come back later, when you have had time to think things over, or to talk them through with someone close to you. If you are not happy with the first undertaker you contact, try another.

If you are a member of a church or other religious group, the funeral rites and the person officiating will be known to you, and you will have the loving support of the other members. All these things can help in making the funeral a ceremony with some meaning. Many people are not part of an established church or group, but would like to have a religious service for a loved one. In practise, this usually means the Church of England service, conducted by the vicar in whose parish the deceased lived. If you and the deceased are not known to the vicar, he will want to find out something of the life and interests of the deceased, to use in his address. You could also ask if someone who is well known to you, and who would like to, could speak. If the Church of England service seems not to be what you want, you could try approaching someone from one of the other liberal churches, such as the Unitarian. You could devise your own ceremony in consultation with the appropriate official and the undertaker. Remember, it is your choice.

If you have no religious affiliation but would like a ceremony which is simple and beautiful, there are Humanist Associations who will help and will send an officiant if you would like one. They have literature they will send at a modest cost.

If, after all, you feel that circumstances have pushed you into a ceremony which was impersonal and unsatisfying, then you can hold a memorial meeting afterwards if you would like to. The form it takes, the place, time and date, will be up to you and those close to you.

You might feel that your grief cannot be so shared, but there is a need to mark the passing of your loved one in some special way, perhaps quite privately. Plant a tree, perhaps? Take flowers to a favourite place? Try not to be inhibited from saying goodbye in your own way, for fear of being thought odd. We should not let convention rob us of the expression of deep and important feelings. A loving farewell is often an important step in the progress of grief. A funeral rite, whatever form it takes, should assist the living to take that step, so it needs to be meaningful, relevant and individual.

9

Practical considerations

Money

The last thing that someone newly bereaved wants to be thinking about is money. It is hard to come to grips with the everyday necessities when the mind and heart are so occupied elsewhere. Memory and concentration are often badly affected by bereavement too, so that working sums out is doubly difficult. It can also feel like a betrayal of the loved one, to be thinking about money so soon. However, it cannot be left to chance or neglected — the practical needs of the survivor must be met.

Some people are financially better off after bereavement but many are not. The grim but necessary task of working out the financial position will not go away. Even when it feels as though the world has come to an end, the bills keep on arriving, reminding us that it has not. As soon as it can be faced, the job of looking at the cold realities of the future must be attended to. It is vital to know how much there will be to live on, and how to manage any change in one's position. No doubt anyone faced with such a task will have a super-abundance of advice from all and sundry, and all of it well-meant. It may be that one needs to listen and give due consideration to all, but also to consult a detached professional like a bank manager or accountant. One big advantage of so doing is that facts and figures will need to be marshalled, and that in itself can begin to make some order out of chaos. It need not all be done at once and in a rush, but can be worked on as and when concentration allows. It is not a disservice to the dead to consider the needs of the living.

First, then, it is important to know what your income will be, and what your outgoings are, and to look at any changes that may need to be made. Some income may be lost, but you may now be cooking for only one, or be entitled to benefit.

The organization Cruse (see useful addresses) produces helpful fact-sheets on budgeting (and some branches arrange cash-and-carry buying of foods at a discount to members). Cruse provides a great deal of practical help as well as emotional support.

Food

Shopping for one can take time to get used to; it is common for people to forget in the early stages of grief, and to go on buying the same amount as before. Warming things up for a second time may not be very appealing, particularly when mood and interest are low. It is so easy to become discouraged and not to bother. However, ill-health can result from neglecting the diet, so ways need to be found to combat the problem. At various stages of my life, I have met with groups of friends for lunch or supper. Sometimes the hostess provides all the meal, sometimes it is a co-operative effort; once a week, once a month, same venue or going to a different one each time, or finding a cheap place to eat out. Sometimes these occasions have arisen from misfortune or necessity, but sometimes from the pleasure of having someone to cook for (or the pleasure of being cooked for!). There has been no difference in the enjoyment of a shared meal, however it arose. There are, of course, formal luncheon clubs, but these too originally grew from need or friendship. Often, when a person alone might have 'managed' with a bit of bread and some tinned soup, a guest provides the impetus for something a little special, and it need not be expensive. This can be as true for an elderly widower as a young widow with children — anyone now alone.

Guests, of course, cannot come every day, and preparing food just for one can seem like too much of a chore on some days. Good wholesome food, however, does not necessarily need elaborate preparation or even cooking. Now that canned and frozen foods are labelled with information about nutritive values, and there are vacuum-packed and chill-fresh whole meals available too, convenience meals can be easy *and* good for you. Salads and fresh fruit, good wholemeal bread and cheese, can be assembled in minutes and cause very little washing up — an added bonus when energy is low. Cruse (address on page 121) has useful information on cooking, and some branches organize discounted bulk buying for members. Groups of friends and neighbours can also use this facility to save money.

Saving time, energy and money is good, but it is important to serve the food attractively, even if there is no one to see it but you. Piling things together anyhow, or eating straight out of the tin, can be the first step on the slippery slope of real self-neglect — and it is a hard road back from there.

The home

Many people feel the need to get away for a few days after the funeral, but most pine to be home again soon. The familiar four walls and furniture, and the bits and pieces around belonging to the loved one, are often a comfort. Someone recently told me that she knew the house was now too big, 'But I shan't move yet,' she said, 'I feel his presence there, and it is good.' Indeed, unless a change of home is inevitable, it is not a good idea to undergo a major upheaval like moving, soon after bereavement. Moving itself is very disruptive, and anyone still in the throes of grief is most unlikely to settle in a new home. The depression and other bad feelings will come with you. If it is possible, leave it at least a year; give time to sort out the old clothes and the possessions no longer needed, and time to feel that the future can look promising again.

What friends can do

In difficult and confusing situations, when we feel particularly stressed, most people have a tendency to cling on to old patterns of behaviour. There is comfort in the usual routine, particularly when everything around feels as if it is in turmoil, or no one is sure what the future holds. However, after any significant change through loss, new ways have to be learned, as some of the old ones have now become inappropriate. Learning to be single again, instead of half of a couple, is perhaps one of the hardest things to do. It also appears to be hard for other people to adapt to the changed state of things judging by the many painful accounts from widows and widowers, who can so easily be made to feel that they are a social embarrassment.

For example, perhaps people who say, 'You must come round for coffee sometime,' without specifying when, fail to realize that such a vague invitation can cause pain. Perhaps in former days, the recipient would have said, 'Okay, when?' Now, after being bereaved, that same person may be feeling very uncertain about himself or herself, and a vague message like that can make someone suspect that it is not really sincere. Self-esteem is often shaky for a long time after bereavement, and a feeling that the world neither wants nor needs you now is easy to propagate. Presumably, the intention is not to wound someone already in pain. It is more likely that the inviter feels awkward in the new situation, and wants to say something friendly but is afraid of making a blunder. 'Suppose I invite him/her for coffee? I will have to make conversation. Will I make a mess of it? Should I talk about the dead person or not? I don't know. I want to be kind, but I could end by making things worse.' It is probably that kind of approach/avoidance conflict, together with a poor understanding of the bereaved person's new lack of confidence, which causes the problem. It need not be so difficult. As Schulman and Rehm point out,[15] the actual words are less important than the very presence of another caring person. The most highly-valued person to someone bereaved is not the one who expresses most sympathy, but the one who stays around and makes few demands.

Making few demands would mean *not* leaving the initiative about fixing dates and times to the invitee, but suggesting them yourself. It means *not* fretting about what you should nor should not talk about, which can create a tense, uncomfortable atmosphere, but simply being your old familiar self — natural and unforced. Above all, it means being a listening ear, and realizing that advice is not needed unless it is specifically asked for, and that a hug or a pat on the hand can be worth a thousand words. Your bereaved friend does not need someone else to think for them, just your affection and uncritical support.

Sometimes there is also a feeling of awkwardness in that it is felt that someone getting over grief might not want to do the old familiar social things, in case they are reminded of times past, and made sad. This may be true, but on the other hand, the time comes when old memories can bring happiness too. In either case, it is better to ask how someone feels about doing things, rather than leaving them out or making arrangements so vague that they are not sure whether they are included or not. Even if the note or call of invitation results in a refusal, they will know that someone has been thinking of them, and that can mean a great deal. However it makes them feel, it cannot be as bad as feelings engendered by being left out altogether.

Another demand we sometimes unwittingly make of the bereaved is to treat them like objects of pity. Again, when self-esteem is low anyway, to be pitied can confirm the 'poor thing' feeling. Feeling for someone is quite different from feeling sorry for someone. It is important to avoid giving the impression that someone is being included in an invitation simply because he or she is alone. That can be as offensive as being left out altogether.

In the normal course of events, we extend invitations to people who are likeable, fun, interesting, or to those we would like to get to know better. Those same people do not stop being one or all of those things after loss. Sometimes, of course, a bereaved person or couple is not fun just now, and may even be hard to like for a while. They were pleasant once, and will no doubt be so again. Friends take each other for better or worse. If we did not see each other through the bad times, we might never learn to perfect the important human skills like tolerance, patience and kindness.

In deciding whether to include someone in a social event, perhaps it is more important to ask if they feel like a lot of company just now, and if the answer is no, it would be better to ask them alone or with just one or two other familiar people.

Facing another person's grief can teach us about ourselves and our strengths and weaknesses. We need the sad people as much as they need us.

Taking the initiative

If you have been bereaved, going into the new phase of life can be made easier by the care and concern of those around, but ultimately it is a question of individual responsibility. The world may or may not beat a path to your door, but it is still all out there waiting for you. You cannot undo the tragedy of the loss, but perhaps you can prevent it becoming a worse one by preventing the loss of that life from ruining other lives, beginning with your own.

Others may want to approach you, but not know how to make the first move. Perhaps their embarrassment appears like unfriendliness, so you do not approach them, and so you reach an impasse. To break it, you could start by asking yourself which is the most likely — that they feel awkward or are being unfriendly for no reason that you know of? What is the most likely explanation for their behaviour? If it really seems like unfriendliness, perhaps it is best not to pursue them. It is their loss too. However, it will usually not be the case. Can judgement and criticism be suspended, then, and *needs* attended to instead?

June Emerson[16] describes how a male neighbour felt unable to approach her mother after her father's death. One day he was outside the house talking to someone who was washing the car. The mother was making coffee, and rather than drink hers alone, she called him in for a cup. Once that first awkwardness was got over by one of them, the old friendship could be renewed. Conventional wisdom might say that it was his 'place' to make the first move. However, he was not able to, so out with convention and in with the need to find a solution, rather than let the unhappy situation go on.

One courageous woman, bereaved soon after moving to a new neighbourhood, and with school-age children, knocked on the door of a woman in the same street, with children at the same school. 'I need help,' she said, quite simply. 'I need to work, and I have to leave early in the morning. Will you take my children to school with yours?' 'Yes,' said the woman, taken aback but not offended by the direct approach. 'Good. Thank you. Now, what can I do for you in return?', asked the widow. 'Shall I pick them all up from school and give you a break?' It took courage, but it paid off magnificently. Everyone benefited, and new friendships were formed.

These early excursions into renewed or brand-new relationships and activities are trial-and-error at first, and can go wrong. Sometimes we can be pushed into things too soon by other people, or by a feeling that we 'ought to have got over it by now'. There is a particular danger of this happening as depression lifts, and energy and interest begin to return. This phase is often thought to be the end of mourning, both by the mourners and those around them. However, it is unlikely that this is so, particularly if it occurs during the first year of bereavement. A good guide is to consider how emotionally fragile you seem to be, compared with what you were like before you were bereaved, and how well your memory and concentration seem to be working at present. If you think they are not what they were, or you are not sure, then it may not yet be time to make decisions that cannot easily be undone. That time will come, but it is not here yet. As an example of this, Harari[17] studied the reactions of six doctors' widows, who had been referred to him for what was considered to be pathological grief. The widows had all had husbands with chronic illnesses, and had been very heavily involved in their care. A lot was expected of them. After their husbands had died, the widows recalled feelings of some relief, followed by a powerful awareness of their own great weariness. However, within a few months, as energy began to return, each of them tried to pick up the threads and get on with their lives. They went back to work, or planned a holiday or tried to resume a pastime or membership of a club or organization. These activities tended to be brought to a stop rapidly by a variety of symptoms such as irritability, insomnia, headaches, weakness and moodiness, which persisted over time. In these cases, the grief had not been dealt with fully, and had become a problem over and above what would be normally expected.

It is clear that very many people push themselves, or are pushed by others, into 'getting on with life' too soon. Of course, it is sensible to take the opportunity to begin again when one feels able, and there is the fear that if one fails to do so, one might never get back to normal. However, trying too soon can be demoralizing when it ends in failure. Those who have been bereaved should feel at least physically recovered and reasonably predictable emotionally before trying any major new venture, and then you should not try too much at once. Build confidence in one or two things first, to give you a stable base to go on from. The length of time it takes to get to this stage is a very individual thing which will vary widely with circumstances, but it will seldom be less than a year for full recovery.

There are some excellent and helpful accounts from personal experience of the process of learning to live again after bereavement. They are mostly written by widows, and I have included a list at the end of the book. (See further reading.)

A key factor in the resolution of mourning is that, although other people, with their needs of us and ours of them, seem to determine what we think, feel and do to a large extent, there is still a central core of the self which is relatively inviolable. For example, our capacity to care and to cope remains the same, even if the main channel for its expression is no longer there. The loss of a love-object does not reduce the capacity to love, it remains the same as ever. After bereavement and grief, it must find new outlets and, perhaps, other modes of expression, but it is still intact. The world is full of indomitable people who have been bereaved, who have, on the resolution of their grief, channelled their skills, energies and caring into something new and good.

A new life

Bereavement often takes away the future we might have had, but it does not take away the future itself. When grief is over, it is time to take a look at life as it is *now*. How much of your taken-for-granted daily routine is really relevant to how you live now. What needs to change to help you to adapt to the here-and-now, and enable you to look to the future? How do you spend your time now? If you find time often lies heavy on your hands, how could things change so that it is filled *well* for you? The time comes round to ask all these questions. It may not come very quickly. For many people, the seasons and the old anniversaries and festivals will have come and gone at least once before a new future can realistically be faced, but the time does come.

In becoming part of another person, particularly one half of a couple, or a parent, we gain some things and lose others. Independence? Competence, perhaps? After being the wife of a super-efficient man for many years, I have forgotten how to change fuses. An article in a newspaper suggested that many elderly widowers were in rest homes and the like, not because of illness but because they never learned to wash their own socks . . . it's a sobering thought. Now may be the time to look at those aspects of ourselves which have remained undeveloped or have become withered, and see what we want to change.

By focusing on some relationships, we may exclude others. By being enfolded within a family we may become blinkered to a range of other possibilities. After grief is done, we may be in a position to think again, and begin to explore some of those possibilities.

New activities

In Betty Jane Wylie's book *Beginnings*[18] she suggests that a start in making a new life could be 'filling in the lonely gaps'. This means identifying and listing the difficult parts of the week. Perhaps they are the times not filled up with enjoyable or purposeful activities, or those which were once shared with the one you have lost. No doubt there are people only too ready to tell you what you *ought* to be doing during those times, but it is more to the point to do what you *want* to do. If you have never been a joiner of clubs before, it is unlikely that you will suddenly change now. Perhaps you have always been reserved. Bereavement is not likely to turn you into a raging extrovert. The need for the company of others, in amount and type, is a very personal thing, and only you can decide what your needs are, although you might want to bounce ideas off a trusted close friend or relative.

One strategy might be to make a list of things you would like to do, or always meant to try, and then to look at how practical they are. How much time, money and energy are likely to be involved? Will they fit in with other important things in your life?

Talk things over with someone you trust, and who knows you well, and then begin to try one or two things out. It might be better to start with things that are not too difficult or too important. It may be that not everything works out in the way that you had hoped, but try not to get discouraged. This is trial-and-error time. You may not have lived like this since adolescence, when it was probably fun to go to different things just to see what they were like. This is a second chance to experiment, alone or with a friend.

New relationships

Inevitably, if you have been one half of a couple, and had a loving relationship, coming back into the social world will bring you face to face with the need for physical love and affection. There might have been a time when that need seemed to have faded, but the need is probably still there. Other people may get there ahead of you, and assume that you are in need of a sexual relationship. Many widows report being made 'offers' to, often by married men, and often the husbands of long-standing friends. At best, these are clumsy but kindly meant gestures designed to comfort and console; at worst, they masquerade as that but are in reality opportunities for lust, not love. Even with the best motives, however, such overtures frequently give great offence. First, because just as it took time to learn to be married, it takes time to learn to be unmarried again. It isn't easy to get used to the idea of being single. Faithfulness to the memory of the lost one can last a long time, and run deep. When this is so, a sexual proposition can seem both immoral and painful (even if the propositioner is free). Secondly, perhaps there *is* a strong desire that needs fulfilling. Someone who has been used to a close loving relationship in which needs for affection and sex were regularly mutually satisfied, is unlikely to be able to turn the need off. This is not something public, however, and it can be shocking to have a need with which one is having a private struggle, exposed in that way — particularly if the person offering to meet it is someone you do not feel drawn to. Third, although there might be a strong need for physical affection and sexual release, the emotional complications of becoming entangled with someone inappropriate are something the bereaved person can well do without. After a struggle with grief, no one needs another emotional upheaval so soon.

No doubt the time will come when you know whether you are ready for a new relationship. Not everyone feels that need. Those who do find new partners and who are successful and happy will probably have allowed themselves time to feel whole and strong again, before embarking on this new venture. In the meantime, what to do about sexual tension? Distraction can often work well, particularly if it involves physical exercise of some kind and self-release (masturbation) is a safe form of sexual activity, free from emotional and physical risks. Of course, none of these may be a proper substitute for a mutual expression of physical love, but until the right time comes, they may be better than nothing at all or sex with risks attached.

Whether or not sex itself is an issue, someone who has lost a partner is vulnerable. Some people fear a new relationship, as the loss of the first one was so painful that even the remote possibility of a new loss seems too much to bear. Usually, this fear passes with time, but if it does not, counselling or some other form of professional help should be sought. Fear should not be allowed to cut anyone off from the potential joys and benefits of a new relationship. Not that everyone will need or want a new marriage or partnership, but that choice should be based on reason, not fear.

At the other extreme from someone phobic about new relationships is the person desperately afraid of being alone, unloved, unsought, and clutching at any straw that chance blows by. Loneliness may seem like the worst thing, but being vulnerable to exploitation is the worst part of it. Fragile self-esteem can be destroyed by the discovery that one has been used. Bring the new person into your life. Invite them to meet trusted friends and family, and get their reaction. When tempted by the prospect of a casual sexual encounter, ask yourself how you'll feel in the morning, or in a month's time, when you look back. Try to take time to think about what you are doing to yourself, and bounce ideas off a close friend or counsellor. Don't be hasty to become heavily involved too soon, or to part with material possessions which are important to your financial stability. A good relationship will last, so you have plenty of time to let it develop. If it isn't good, do you really want to stay involved? Anything that feels rushed is suspect, and you are probably better to let it go, and be sad now rather than overwrought later.

You have already had the chance to find out that all your capacity for caring and coping is intact. It is an essential part of you, and it can survive loss. That goes on being true, and practising those skills is important. Start by practising them on yourself. Self-care is essential before good strong relationships with other people can be formed. If you treat yourself like a doormat, other people will accept the invitation to walk on you.

10

Letting go and learning to live separately

After the turmoil of early grief is over, and unfamiliar moods have come and gone, most people come to realize that they are feeling like their old self again. They will not have forgotten the loved one, but will have accepted the loss. Grief has served its purpose and allowed the process of adjustment to go on. Now it is time to let go of grief. This is not always easy to do, and can sometimes feel like a betrayal of the loved one — as if their death took away the right of the survivor to be happy. Intellectually, we know this is nonsense, but feelings don't always obey the rules of the intellect. The time comes when reluctance to end grieving needs challenging, however. What purpose is being served by going on mourning? It achieves nothing but torture of the self. C.S. Lewis has argued convincingly that prolonged mourning keeps the dead away from us; sorrow blankets us from them; they cannot live fully in the memory until that sorrow is released.

Sometimes a misplaced sense of loyalty keeps grief alive. Someone recently said, 'I owe it to her.' But what do we owe those we love? Surely the acknowledgement of all they gave us while alive. Loving relationships are strengthening; we build on them. They become absorbed into the positive, healthy aspects of the self. None of that can be taken away by death. Part of our capacity to be happy comes from the experience of loving and being loved. Death cannot take it away. We can pay no better tribute to the dead than to use the attributes they had a part in forming, to the full. Imagine how you would feel if all you had bequeathed to a loved one was the ability to mourn. If all your influence had not helped them to be positive, happy, loving, forward-looking, what a waste of life that would be. Letting go of grief is an affirmation of love, not a betrayal.

Sometimes, though, grief cannot be let go. The dead person is enshrined, and the survivor is chained to the shrine. An over-close relationship can sometimes produce the problem, particularly if it has excluded others. A relationship which has been close but ambivalent can also prolong the grieving process as it has so much unfinished emotional business tangled up with it. There may be a sense almost of being haunted by the loss. The survivor may be unable to sort out and dispose of old clothes and other possessions; unable to discuss the dead person without exaggerating their good qualities so that they sound like saints or angels; unable to discuss them at all, perhaps, because it remains too painful. On the other hand, they may be unable to keep them out of conversation, so great is their preoccupation. If these hang-ups persist beyond a reasonable time, which may be eighteen months or two years, it is time to consider getting skilled help, as they are unlikely to resolve themselves spontaneously after that time.

The majority of people will not be affected like this. They will find that grief resolves, slowly and undramatically. There is no sudden revelation; rather, a growing sense of purpose and wholeness, and a dawning realization of happiness, like a quietly progressive thaw after a long winter. The resolution of grief is aided by allowing oneself the time and space to mourn at the time of loss. Sometimes the most capable member of the family is so busy looking after everyone else that their own grief has to be suppressed. Sometimes others inhibit them from showing grief. 'Don't upset yourself,' or 'This is not like you.' Sometimes others over-protect, keeping someone from the death-bed, the body, the funeral, thus giving little chance for reality to be grasped. All these things can cause a hold-up in the natural flow of feelings, which may cause problems later. Grief held back has not gone away. We do now understand the process of grief, and the need for those who are grieving to be able to feel and express it fully and freely. When that is allowed to happen, resolution and letting go will be possible in the end.

11

Losing a baby or infant

Miscarriage

Miscarriage is not uncommon. It has been estimated that at least 1 in 10 pregnancies end in this way. They are not usually life-threatening to the mother, and a rapid, straightforward method of dealing with the physical aftermath has been developed. It is the usual practice to admit the woman to hospital, perform a D. and C. (dilatation and curettage) to remove any of the 'products of conception' which might be retained in the uterus and cause problems later, and send her home a few hours later or the next day when she has recovered from the general anaesthetic. If a miscarriage is 'threatened', which is usually heralded by bleeding, she may be advised to rest at home or admitted to hospital. Once the miscarriage becomes inevitable, usually because the cervix has opened fully, the procedure described above will follow.

A woman who has had a miscarriage will be unlikely to be offered anything in the way of formal support and counselling. If hers is an unusual case, such as in multiple miscarriage, or if a treatable condition such as inadequate cervix is diagnosed, she will be followed up medically and anything which might prevent a recurrence will be offered to her. However, the brief existence of the lost baby is unlikely to be recognized as a significant event by hospital staff, and in only a very few places will the need for grief counselling be acknowledged.

Most miscarriages occur in the early weeks and months of pregnancy, before the baby is developed enough to survive outside the womb. The pregnancy may hardly have been acknowledged by those outside the immediate family circle, before it is suddenly over. Sometimes there is no warning; sometimes the mother may suspect that all is not well. She may keep this fear to herself and hope that it will pass, or she may have been told to rest by a family doctor. If the miscarriage is going to happen, it usually presents itself as a flood of heavy bleeding, which often carries the tiny foetus away with it unseen, if it occurs early in pregnancy.

After miscarriage, the question 'Why?' is bound to be asked, and in most cases there will be no clear answer. It is often supposed that miscarriages are nature's way of ejecting a non-viable foetus, but that is more of a supposition than an established fact at present. In an otherwise normal healthy woman, little thought is given to the reason for a miscarriage. The mother will usually be told to try again after three months.

None of this efficient mechanism for dealing with a fairly common, non-life-threatening (to the mother) event takes into account the idea that a baby has been lost. Perhaps it was a longed-for child; perhaps it was conceived after a lot of difficulty and a long wait, and seen as an only hope for a couple; perhaps it was one of a series of babies lost this way, with despair of a pregnancy ever going to full term and producing a live child increasing each time. Often, it will be the first pregnancy of a young woman with all her hopes and dreams before her. Perhaps it was an 'accidental' or unwanted pregnancy, with a tangle of confused feelings associated with it. If the miscarriage occurs later in the pregnancy, the mother might have felt the baby move, and perhaps there has been speculation about its sex, and names chosen.

Because the onset is usually sudden and the hospital's way of dealing with it so rapid, the mother may easily go home afterwards in a state bordering on unreality; it was all over so quickly that it seems like a bad dream. However, grief for the child lost as the result of miscarriage is common and very real. Studies have shown that transient periods of grief do occur after miscarriage, although prolonged or pathological grieving is mercifully rare.

In the days following, feelings of guilt are common, together with great anxiety about what could have gone wrong. Was it something she did? There may also be feelings of anger — perhaps the doctors could have done more? These feelings are often shared by both parents, as are pangs of sadness and longing for the lost baby. These may not come immediately, but may be delayed for a few days or a significant length of time;

perhaps until the baby would have been born.

In the vast majority of cases, the opportunity to express and share all these feelings freely, will be the most helpful way to work through grief. It is also important to ask about any concerns for future pregnancies, so a talk with the family doctor can be useful. With regard to the future, perhaps there will be another baby, but it will not be a substitute or replacement for the lost one. It will be a new and different child. The lost one needs its share of grief, however much it is, however long it takes, and then it needs to be let go and the grief put behind. Fortunately, grief after a miscarriage is not usually prolonged, particularly if the grief has been acknowledged and shared. Often, a loving partner, a sympathetic friend or doctor, will provide the needed support, counselling and sharing of feelings. Reassurance is more important than advice or opinion.

If there is no one who can provide these things, you could contact one of the relevant groups listed on page 117; enquire at your local health clinic, or ask your doctor to put you in touch with a counsellor or psychologist. Do not be afraid to ask for help. It was not nothing that you lost, and your need to grieve is not abnormal.

Abortion

Most articles in magazines fail to make much of an impression. One or two seem to stick in the mind for a very long time. Such a one was an account I once read of a woman's experience of abortion. The reason for the abortion has not stayed with me. In a sense, it does not matter, as her feelings and reactions are the central concern. She talked to the baby in her womb the night before the operation. She said three things. 'Goodbye', 'I'm sorry', and 'I hope you get a better mother next time.' Sorrow, regret and hope. That woman was articulate, unusually so perhaps, and in touch with her own feelings. Many women are not, and too few are given any kind of chance to be.

Rather like suicide, abortion runs counter to most people's rather cosy view of what the world ought to be like, and how people ought to feel, think and behave. We ought to love and want babies. We ought not to get pregnant unless we want to, or unless we are in the appropriate social position to care for the baby. When these 'oughts' fail to happen, a lot of uncomfortable challenges are generated, along with feelings of hostility towards those who generate them.

Our present abortion law, seen by some people as forward thinking and humane, is viewed by others with horror, and as a licence to kill. Because personal belief rather than objective fact fuels the debate, it seems unlikely that it will ever be resolved. It is right that the debate should go on, and that we should take nothing for granted.

In the meantime, however, there is the dilemma facing someone seeking abortion for medical or social reasons. No amount of medical expertise will make abortion an 'easy' option for most women. The decision to end a pregnancy is often taken against a background of pain and conflict. The hard-faced or carefree woman seeking an easy way out is probably an extreme rarity, if not altogether a fictional character. As Beverley Raphael has pointed out,[19] we do not know what proportion of women experience a period of grief, mourning and guilt, and what proportion resolve the issue of their abortion relatively easily. We do not know because definitive studies have not been carried out. However, the complex background to most, if not all abortions, and the negative attitudes of many people towards abortion for any reason, give grounds for the suspicion that it will be a difficult time for most women. For those who are supported in their decision by the baby's father, close family members, friends and professionals, things might be easier than for those facing it alone. The opportunity to talk through feelings of guilt and anguish, sharing responsibility for the decision, and receiving reassurance, can only be helpful. The need to grieve will often be important, and where this is understood, and its expression encouraged, this can also ease the path. Those women who lack support, or who go through the whole process in secret, or who are hardly out of their own childhood before facing the double traumas of pregnancy and abortion, are probably most at risk. It is becoming usual for counselling to be offered to any woman before abortion, and some health authorities offer follow-up, particularly for the young single woman. No matter how strongly it may be felt that abortion is a tragedy, it should not be allowed to become a double tragedy. The loss of one life cannot be paid for by the ruin of another. Whatever the reason for the loss, a woman who has lost a baby is likely to need that loss acknowledged and attended to, and should be encouraged to seek help if need be.

The Marie Stopes Clinic will assist women in Britain who need emotional help after abortion (address on page 117) if no appropriate local service is available.

Stillbirth and perinatal death

The mother who gives birth to a dead child, or one which dies soon after, is plunged from the prospect of joy to the reality of grief in a particularly cruel way. Even those who have known or suspected that the baby will not be born alive may still hope, and the death will not become a reality for them until birth makes it manifest. Society has been slow to get to grips with the needs of people who have been bereaved in this way, but in recent years much valuable work has been done in clinical research and in the formation of groups such as the Stillbirth and Neonatal Death Society. The importance of early care for the parents and the significance of acknowledging the child by seeing it, holding it, giving it a name, and acknowledging its death in funeral rites, are now understood. That grief which is not allowed to be expressed can go on to influence future life, relationships and children as yet unborn, is also known and this knowledge can be used.

In their chapter on Stillbirth in *Death and Dying, A Quality of Life*[20] Hazelanne Lewis and Judith Liston make the observation that there is no space for a first name on the certificate of burial of a stillborn child. This is a sad comment on society's official attitude to stillbirth, which hardly acknowledges that a unique human being was alive, even for so short a time, in the womb. The authors point out that the Registrar can be asked to write the name in above the surname. They stress the importance of naming the child. Naming denotes its existence and personal uniqueness. No child can be replaced by another, as some well-meaning people suggest. This one has been lost; a later one is a separate entity. This one needs its share of grief, and then needs to be let go, so that undealt-with emotion does not go on to cloud the future.

In past years, and still sometimes today, there has been a tendency for a baby born dead to be whisked out of the delivery room with indecent speed before parents see it, particularly if it is not perfectly formed or if it has died sometime before delivery. The parents may then never see their child. Now that we understand more about the nature of loss and grief, we know the importance of seeing the body in accepting the reality of death. Death is hard to accept, particularly if it is sudden, and more so when it is involved with birth. We cannot easily get to grips with something when its reality has been blurred.

Studies have shown that parents are helped in their grief by being shown their baby, and, if the way is prepared for them, they will usually ask to do so. Occasions on which it is not felt possible or advisable because of mutilation or deformity are mercifully rare and should get specialist counselling and follow-up.

When parents are told about the baby — its sex, the colour of its hair and so on, and their questions are answered, they are more likely to want to see and perhaps hold their child than if information is not given and they imagine the worst. Accounts of the experiences of parents with their dead babies have tended to show that they look on the little ones with the eyes of love, not the eyes of clinical experience. Many parents who decide not to see their babies go on to regret it bitterly later, and to suffer unduly as a consequence. It is not a 'must',of course, and there are sometimes special circumstances which make it inadvisable, but in the main, gentle encouragement to do so is the right thing. In her moving account of her own experience, *Nobody Told Me*[13] Christine Simpson, whose baby was born by Caesarean section and died very soon afterwards, tells how she declined to see and hold her child. She was clearly in a state of shock then, and remained so after discharge. She found that she could not plan a meal properly any more, or shop without forgetting half of it. She became panicky and would not go out. She was subject to violent emotions, particularly anger, and wanted to throw bricks through babyshop windows. She had fears for her own sanity, and became withdrawn. Feelings of emptiness took her over. Finally, she contacted the hospital, which had a photograph of her baby, and asked them to send it. When she got her baby's photo, she was at last able to cry tears of utter sadness, and to know that there *had* been a baby, and that it was lost to her. That acknowledgement is crucial in assisting a normal grieving process. Christine's story is by no means unique, and its message is clear. The birth/death experience must be made real if it is to be dealt with.

Hospitals will bury a stillborn baby free of charge, and will make all the arrangements. Shocked parents will often agree to this before they have had time or space to think clearly about it, and will often fail to ask for details at the time. One young couple were distressed to find that their child had been buried without their knowledge in a communal grave with rows of other tiny coffins. They embarked on the lengthy, complicated and expensive process of applying for an exhumation and reburial. Perhaps if it had all been explained to them with more care initially (and written details given too, for preference) and they had been given time to think, they would have been spared that additional suffering. Like so many parents in that situation, they were young and it was their first close encounter with death. It came at a time of joyful preparation for new life, too, which was suddenly swamped by grief instead.

Seeing the dead baby, arranging and attending the funeral, will of course be painful, but that pain is a necessary part of the work of grief, and it is better than emptiness and unacknowledged feelings which can go on to cause problems later. Robert Fulton[21] has carried out a study which showed that where the body was not seen, or arrangements had been made for disposal without a proper funeral or without involving the parents, there was a tendency for hostility and increased anxiety and tension later. Losing a baby cannot be made easy, but it can be made easier than it often is, by using skills and knowledge we already possess.

Astrid Anderson is a hospital chaplain. One of her duties is to conduct funerals for these babies. Sometimes she is alone in the chapel for the service. She writes that she performs the funeral rite as a human being, to show respect to 'the least of His brethren', and by doing so, to show respect for life itself.[20] C.S. Hausman, writing in the same book, points out that the funeral allows sorrow; it helps to bring death home, so that grief can begin; it creates memories. Not least, it tells us that a precious person is gone, not a thing whose disposal does not matter. It does not have to be the funeral service of a particular religion, of course, but however it is planned, it is a powerful and important rite of passage.

The sensitive handling of parents who have lost a baby in this way, needs to start from the time the death is known about, which will be pre-birth in some cases. Usually a bereaved mother refers herself to the Stillbirth and Neonatal Death Society or similar organization after discharge from hospital, but by then difficulties may already have begun, not only those already mentioned here, but others such as being in the Maternity Unit surrounded by other people's babies, but being isolated from them. Earlier contact with SANDS could provide support from the beginning, and through the days following discharge and beyond.

It is often supposed that women get over stillbirth and perinatal death very quickly, particularly if they have other children. This is not so, and the presence of other children can complicate grief, as the parents try to struggle with all the demands on them. Parents may also be urged by others to try again for another baby as soon as possible — again, the idea of 'replacement'. Studies have shown, however, that later babies are more easily accepted than those born eighteen months or less after a neonatal death. Any other children in the family will have their grief too. All these factors can create additional difficulties at an already difficult time, so that the need for skilled and ongoing assistance is vital in order that present suffering is eased and the future is not compromised. Details of the Stillbirth and Neonatal Death Society and other groups are given on page 118.

Cot death

The phenomenon of sudden infant death (cot death) is not new. The fact that apparently healthy babies can die, for no medically ascertainable reason, has been brought into focus with the advent of effective birth control and smaller families. Unlike our forebears, we expect all our children to survive into adulthood and to outlive us. Better health care and advances in health technology mean that mortality from stillbirth and neonatal death has been falling in recent years, but the incidence of cot death has remained curiously static. Unlike perinatal death, which usually occurs in hospital, cot death almost invariably happens at home. Although the age range goes up to two years, most cot deaths occur in babies under six months, so that the bereavement is experienced by parents still emotionally vulnerable after childbirth, and still intensely physically involved with the baby. A mother, in particular, may spend a lot of time cuddling her baby, and even when not doing so, will be attending to its needs in other ways. The intense ache of longing associated with empty arms is acutely distressing. The suddenness, and the usual lack of any explanation for the death, are further complicating factors, as are police involvement and the legal requirements of an inquest.

After most kinds of death, the question, 'Why?' will be asked, and the lack of convincing medical reasons for cot death will often lead to extra feelings of self-doubt, blame and guilt. One mother had just stopped breast-feeding her baby when he died, and was tormented by the possibility that the change had caused his death. Another set of parents had gone out for the evening together, for the first time since the birth, leaving the baby with a sitter. The baby died while they were out. There are many other tragic stories involving fears about what parents did or failed to do. When no answers are forthcoming, the imagination can run wild, particularly while people are in the throes of grief. It is important that reassurance that the death was beyond the control of the parents is given, repeatedly if necessary, and that the parents are encouraged to voice their theories about the cause of death, so that any wrong ideas can be dealt with. In the very first instance, the family doctor or health visitor, who knows the family and has knowledge of the subject, can be an invaluable source of comfort, information, and a listening ear. Parents will need to be reassured, not only about the cause of death, but about the intense and complex feelings they may experience, particularly in the early days. Hearing the baby cry, or finding oneself preparing a feed or laundering clothing, are common in the early days. It is important to know that these are not signs of madness, but only part of the struggle of coming to terms with the unthinkable.

Increased tension between parents after cot death is not uncommon, and sometimes feelings of guilt can be so strong that to share them with anyone else seems impossible, and the parent(s) withdraws from everyone. Other family members, particularly other children, will need their fears and their grief attended to as well, at the very time when their usual counsellors and comforters, their parents, are wrapped up in their own feelings. The family is likely to need an intense amount of support and comfort in the early hours and days, and ongoing counselling and help thereafter, as long-term consequences can be deeply damaging if they are not attended to. Confidence in themselves as parents, and in the health care team, can be badly shaken, as explanations are sought and the possibility that *someone* missed an early sign, comes to the fore. Mothers and fathers have described withdrawing from other children, being afraid to love them too much, now that they have experienced the death of one child. A grandmother also described the same kind of feeling to me, saying, 'I couldn't go through that again for the world, so I keep away from them. It hurts me, but it's better this way.' The cost of these feelings is high in terms of the future happiness of everyone closely concerned. If these fears are not dealt with, they can blight the lives of the family and jeopardize relationships with existing children and future babies. Clearly, there is a need for skilled and compassionate help from the earliest hours and days after the death, and sometimes for months afterwards, to help dispel guilt and fear, to give reassurance about the intensity of feelings associated with this form of bereavement, and to listen, listen and listen again. Many sources of support from friends to Ministers of religion may be of assistance. There are also organizations such as the Foundation for the Study of Infant Deaths which will give support and counselling by telephone and letter, and will put bereaved parents in touch with others in their locality who have also experienced cot death. The Foundation has parent groups, and an individual befriending service. These contacts are often invaluable, as grief can be isolating, and this particularly traumatic kind of loss can cut parents off from others because of feelings of shame and guilt. One of the Foundation's strengths is its band of people who have been through the experience of cot death, and will know what the parents are suffering from first-hand experience. They will know how intense and complex mourning can be, and how long it can take, and they will be ordinary people, just like anyone else, all of which can be helpful.

Some parent groups help to raise money for medical research into cot death, and putting energy into the hope of prevention in the future can also be therapeutic. There is now a breathing monitor with an alarm becoming available as a result of research. (While the root cause of death remains unknown to date, one possible factor is the tendency of some babies to stop breathing while asleep). Other research is also going on, so that one day this peculiarly distressing form of loss may become a thing of the past. In the meantime, the knowledge of the depth and complexity of mourning after cot death is already with us, and increasing numbers of parents are being helped through it with the skill and compassion of others. The family doctor or health visitor will put parents in touch with the Foundation.

Details of this and other groups are also given on page 117. There is a helpful article about the Foundation by Sylvia Limerick in *'Death and Dying, A Quality of Life'*[20].

12

When an older child dies

The death of a child, even one quite grown-up, is often associated with deep and prolonged distress in parents. It is one of the most harrowing forms of bereavement. Just as there is the expectation that babies will be healthy and will live, there is the idea that our children will outlive us, and go on to be part of the future. They are part of our hopes for the future; the part of us that will go on. We endow them with dreams and wishes we may not have fulfilled ourselves. The bond between parents and children is often very strong.

A father once commented on the different kinds of love he felt for his children when they were babies, and when they were older. 'When they are so little', he said, 'You love them in a deep, almost animal sort of way. They are so helpless, and they only have you to depend on for everything. You love them because they are. You can't help yourself. When they are older and can talk, and develop personalities, you love them more as people, as friends.' He went on to speak of his delight in watching these small people grow — part of him, and yet independent and autonomous — and he drew on early memories to explain what definite characters his children had. Things seen in embryonic form in babyhood had gone on to become decided traits later. No doubt these were not all sources of joy to him!

All parents will know the weariness and frustration engendered by battles of will with increasingly independent offspring, and the anger one can feel towards a wilful child. These are normal feelings, and are incorporated into a host of others, positive and negative, which go to make up a close loving relationship. Parents may feel that they should not have been angry just then, on reflection, but there is time to make it right later.

There is a fairy-tale sort of image of ideal parenthood — serene, loving, fair, unruffled — which all parents at some time feel they ought to be, but don't quite make it. From time to time, any parent might feel guilty about falling short of their ideal, no matter how unrealistic it might be, but usually life gives us opportunities to go on trying. When death robs us of those chances, the feelings of inadequacy can be overwhelming.

As I wrote this book, there was a story in the news of a small boy who has been missing for some days. Like many another little child, he was angry because a boat trip had come to an end, and did not want to get out of the boat. When he was finally removed by his parents, he ran off in a temper. He has not been seen since. The parents are bewildered, shocked — and guilty. Even though no one could have foreseen the consequences, and it is hard to see what anyone could have done differently, there is the feeling that it ought not to have happened, and they are responsible. Somehow, if a child is lost, the sense of one's failure to be a 'perfect' parent comes to the fore. The fact that the subjective sense of failure might be unrealistic, as in this case, does not prevent the feeling from being very strong and very painful.

The sense of guilt can pervade the whole family, and sometimes close friends and associates as well. In *Cider with Rosie*[22] Laurie Lee describes how he was often ill as a small child, with spectacular fevers and delirium. He writes that everyone was so busy taking care of him that they failed to notice that his little sister was dying. She slipped quietly away. Even after so many years, he conveys a feeling of some responsibility — he was ill, and so they didn't notice her. His illness was dramatic, but he always got better, while she died without any fuss. It is easy to see that his feeling does not arise because of any wilful act on his part. It is independent of the reality of the case, but the feeling of being somehow at fault because the unthinkable has happened, is often overwhelming. Because death is hard to accept, and the death of a child particularly so, it seems that blame must be apportioned, and those close to the child tend to take it upon themselves in the absence of a more obvious culprit. 'If only I had . . ., If only I hadn't . . .' are painfully common after the death of a child. Sometimes it feels as if there is real cause for guilt. The child is sent to the shops, bought a bike, storms off after a row . . . We know on the one hand that we cannot keep children in sight for ever, particularly as they grow up, but the *feeling* that we should have kept them from any possible danger, watching over them around the clock, contradicts the logic.

Even when loss by death is the result of illness rather than accident, self-reproach is a common feature of grief. Some illnesses are genetic, and manifest themselves in children before anyone has suspected a problem. It may be totally illogical to feel guilty about unknowingly passing on a defective gene, but nevertheless, it happens. Illnesses caused by infection, and diseases like cancer, can also lead to self-blame. The guilt is part of grieving, and usually unrelated to the cause of death in any real sense.

Blame is not always restricted to the self when a child dies. The anger and bitterness generated by untimely death is often projected on to doctors, hospital staff — anyone who was around at the time. The inevitability is too hard to take; if only someone had done something differently, the outcome might have changed. Sometimes there may be a reason for the anger but more often than not it is irrational, as is the bitterness bereaved parents may feel towards other parents or other children in the neighbourhood, who may be seen as less deserving of life than the one who died. These feelings pass, but they can be very strong in the early weeks.

When an only child is lost, pining may be a very intense feature of grief. When there are other children, the confusion of feelings and behaviour in their parents can affect them badly, particularly as they will be trying to deal with their own feelings of loss and guilt. Children's emotions can be strong and frightening, and children have been known to fear that their anger towards someone could make them die. Sometimes in quarrels, a child will say, 'Drop dead', or 'I wish you were dead' and it can haunt them later. If the dead child was sick for a time before dying, and had taken up the parents' time and care, brothers and sisters can build up resentment, and that can be hard for them to forgive themselves for later. They may be unable to comfort their parents, and this can make them wonder about the place they hold in parental affection. Everyone loses confidence after bereavement. A surviving child may wonder if the lost one was loved best. After her brother's funeral, which was naturally very emotional, a twelve-year-old said, 'I bet you wouldn't have made all this fuss if I'd died.' It was not simply an angry remark, it was also a plea for reassurance and comfort.

Children may feel that no one acknowledges or understands their grief, because the adults are so wrapped up in their own. They may see their normally reliable parents become apathetic and aimless, and this can be frightening if it is not explained to them by someone. Adolescents, in particular, with their enhanced sensitivity, may find their parents' grief so hard to handle that they cover up their own feelings so as not to cause distress. They may seem nonchalant or even callous. Failing school performance, withdrawal and awkward behaviour may be the only outward signs of grief inside. Such grief needs careful handling, and it may be that someone other than the parents needs to help in the early stages.

Untimely death produces a great sense of personal vulnerability in those closely involved, adults and children alike. Death has come, not in extreme old age, but in the prime of life. If that can happen, then perhaps anything can. The world no longer feels safe. Anyone could be next. Parents may react by becoming fiercely over-protective of their remaining children, or each other; children may react by becoming extra anxious or timid. Teachers, relatives, friends and neighbours can all play a crucial part in providing noncritical sensitive care, and opportunities to talk through feelings. Anyone who feels unable to, or is not chosen to by the bereaved, may find another role to play in providing meals or doing the shopping. Taking some of the practical burdens off bereaved shoulders can be invaluable until they are able to take up the yoke again.

There are no easy answers to offer those bereaved of children; it is a bitterly hard loss. In the very long term, people may be able to regard their lost child as safe from all further harm and pain. One mother was able to say that she felt oddly released in the end — the dreaded, unthinkable thing had happened; nothing could ever be so awful again. These are quotations from parents a long time on, however.

In the early days after the death, someone who understands that loss from personal experience, and who will be there to reassure and to listen, and who will know about the room kept the same, the reluctance to part with clothes and toys; someone who understands the value of reminiscence, and will help to recall the happy times as well as the tragedy; someone like that can be invaluable. The Compassionate Friends is an organization of bereaved parents, who will offer friendship and understanding to others, for as long as it is needed. They will get in touch by telephone, letter, or personal visit. GP surgeries, health visitors, hospitals, Citizen's Advice Bureaux, the Samaritans and the clergy, will all have their leaflets, and will refer parents to them. Referral should be sooner rather than later, although at any stage it can be helpful. Many parents have found the help of Compassionate Friends to be a turning-point in the journey through grief. Some go on to become Friends themselves. Charmion Mann[23] describes the befriending process as accompanying bereaved parents as they make the journey from death to life, and it is, of course, a journey the Friends have made themselves, so they will be skilled guides.

13

Children and bereavement

Very young children

Before children are old enough to speak, the impact of losing someone close to them and important to them cannot be known; it can only be guessed at. It may be that if one warm, loving person is replaced by another, very little impression is made on a small baby. If, on the other hand, the loss of one central person is followed by a procession of different people, and there is inconsistency of care and disrupted routine, it can be surmised that the child will be unsettled and will suffer.

Another important factor in adjustment to loss, is how the child learns about the death of a mother, father or sibling, in later life. A half-explained or badly told story can have a significant effect. Many adults who were bereaved early in life experience difficulties related to that bereavement later. It may be that other family members were wrapped up in their grief, and not able to attend to the emotional needs of a very young child. It may be that there was unresolved anger and bitterness around in those early years, and there was an effect on the care of the child because of it. Sometimes, babies and small children go into local authority or other kinds of care for a while after a bereavement. Any of these things can leave a legacy of uncertainty.

When the loss of a significant other person occurs before there is a conscious memory of that person, there may come a time in later life when the bereaved child feels a great need to seek out relatives with photographs or stories to tell. If the needs are not met, the seeker may become distressed and anxious. Lack of information becomes readily translated into 'mystery', and can cloud relationships with surviving relatives. People may be told not to dig up the past, and not to ask elderly relatives about the dead person, as it might upset them. It is sometimes hard for others to believe how important the search can be, but experiences in clinical practice suggest that it can be crucial. Often, it is a further loss in adult life which triggers the need to make sense of an early bereavement. The need is no less strong because the loss occurred very early in life. If people are helped with finding the necessary information, it is common for them to report feelings such as peace of mind, and a heightened sense of self-worth. The love and pride with which people show photographs, or recount histories, of parents or brothers or sisters they do not consciously remember, is very moving. The diffuse sense of sadness and anxiety which can be experienced by those whose search for information has been blocked or fruitless, is also very striking.

In children as young as fourteen months, signs of acute distress and searching behaviour have been noted after bereavement, which may persist for days or sometimes weeks, but which eventually seem to die away. It is hard to give any meaningful explanation to small children; their vocabulary is limited, and their understanding of time stretching into the future is not established. 'For ever' might as well be 'next week'. One small boy wandered restlessly around the house for days after his father died, calling 'dada, dada', in great distress. There was little to tell him that meant anything, except that Daddy had gone, and little to be done except the comfort and consolation of being held close while he sobbed. In a simple way, this mirrors the best approach to adult bereavement. The best kind of helper is the one who is there and also stays the course and offers comfort. A cuddle can do more than words in adult life too. This story demonstrates that little children do also grieve, and that their grief needs to be taken seriously, and assisted. We know that if adults cannot express their feelings for any reason during bereavement, they may be unable to complete the grieving process. This may also be true of children, so the grief of a child must be taken as seriously as that of an adult.

When children are old enough to have conversations with those around them, their thoughts and feelings about death become apparent. They still have no clear idea about permanency, and tend to believe that a dead person is in another place. It may be called Heaven, but children will be concerned about what will be eaten there, what sort of houses people have, and so on. This concreteness in thinking can lead to difficulties when explanations about death are given. One child was told that Jesus had chosen his baby brother to go and live with him. He became concerned about his other brother, 'Jesus won't choose him too, will he? How many boys does He want?' Children have sometimes developed frightening fantasies about God or Jesus coming in the night to take people away. Being told that someone has gone to sleep forever can also, not surprisingly perhaps, provoke bed-time fears. Ghouls and ghosts from television cartoons may also give rise to horrifying fantasies about dead bodies. All these fears need discussing and questions should be answered as simply and truthfully as possible. Where children have had pets like hamsters, and seen them dead, it can be a useful illustration. The child will see that the body looks pretty much the same, but life has gone out of it. This can be used to talk about the body as the place a person or animal lives in. The idea that there is a 'me' or a soul or spirit which leaves the body at death can be helpful. The empty shell or house is no longer needed. Dr Kübler-Ross[23] uses the image of a butterfly, flying free and leaving the empty chrysalis behind. Where the butterfly has gone can be explained in terms of the parents' beliefs.

In times past, it was usual for children to see the dead body and to attend the funeral. I can remember kissing my great-grandfather goodbye in his coffin at about five years old. I was not upset, and thought he was keeping still as a joke — pretending to be asleep. It was strange that the grown-ups were crying, but his death did not seem awful or frightening. I was told that he had died because he had lived a long time and his heart was worn out, so it stopped beating. He did not need his body any more, as his soul had left it and gone to heaven. Children can accept reality when it is made clear and simple, or when they see it and it is explained in terms they understand.

Seeing the body and attending the funeral can all be helpful in this respect, if someone is there to look to their needs and answer questions. There may be good reasons to exclude children from a funeral sometimes, but it will often be better for them to let them attend.

Children may be content with asking and being told very little, or they may come back with persistent questions. They will be affected, not only by the death, but the strange events surrounding it, and the emotions of others. If information is kept from them, or fudged, they will invent explanations for themselves which may be far more upsetting than the truth. They should not be told not to ask about or talk about the one who has died because it will upset other people, as this denies the validity and strength of their own feelings. If adults in the family are too upset to deal with a child's questions and needs, someone else must — a trusted family friend, perhaps, or a relative who feels able to do so.

Children under any form of stress, including bereavement, will often regress to more babyish ways for a while, such as soiling or wetting, sleep disturbance, clinging, baby talk, or messing with their food. They may direct anger at others, become 'naughty', or play in a violent or aggressive way. Adults, too, behave oddly, often childishly, after bereavement, and can be angry for a while. They are struggling to come to terms with something which often feels too hard to cope with. So are children when they are bereaved. They need the same patient, loving care that we expect as adults in times of crisis.

School-age children

Children older than five can sometimes seem remarkably nonchalant in the face of death. They may be told the news, and go off to play with hardly a change of expression. One eight-year-old told a friend, 'It hasn't been a good year. I fell off my bike and cut my knee. That wasn't very good. I broke a special bit of my technical lego. That wasn't good. My Mum died. That wasn't good either. Can you pass me that red wheel for my truck?' It is not that they do not mourn, or that they do not understand. They are at an age when they work many things out for themselves, and do not always check them against an adult's version. They are also taking in information from school and all around, in large amounts, and spending time thinking about it. Their thoughts are more private than those of pre-school children. It may be that they grieve intermittently, in amongst all their other concerns, and that they do not always show their grief readily. Sometimes, the regression seen in younger children goes into reverse in this age-group, and they try to be a substitute grown-up. It is often easy to believe that they are over it, or coping well, when they may be confused and unhappy but fail to show their feelings. This may happen in families where the child is close to the surviving adult(s) but is inhibited by their grief, or wants to keep quiet so as not to add to their troubles, or in families where the child already felt isolated before the loss. We do not know the long-term effects of bereavement in childhood, although some studies suggest that it can lead to depression in later life. We do know enough about bereavement in general, however, to understand that it may not always be obvious to others, but that the loss of someone close and important will always have an effect; that a bereaved person of any age will need comfort and care, the opportunity to express feelings and reminisce, and to have questions answered. If the surviving adults are not able to perform these functions because of their own grief, it is important that someone is able to, so that the child is not left adrift. It is not safe to assume that they are not grieving, even when it may not be obvious.

Teenagers

Bereavement in adolescence can be particularly traumatic, for a number of reasons. The adolescent child may be struggling with an emerging sense of self, with all its uncertainties, and thus be feeling personally vulnerable. Adolescence is often a time of strong emotions which can be felt as overwhelming. Rapid and dramatic body changes can increase anxiety about physical health and mortality. The sense of time stretching into the future, and the apparent rapid ageing of parents can also feel threatening. There is also often a period of family turbulence as the emerging adult becomes self-assertive, with anger and feelings of rejection on both sides as prominent features. It is also characteristically a time when fantasy life is rich and important, and not shared with parents or other family members.

Someone adolescent and struggling with a mixture of strong feelings, may be unable to cope with the grief of parents; it is too threatening. They may not only withdraw from parents, but also keep their own feelings to themselves, or share them only with close peer-group friends.

A study carried out in America[24] showed that feelings of shock, guilt, confusion, depression, loneliness and anger were felt by interviewees at all stages of the study, which carried on for two years after the bereavement, although these feelings tended to diminish in strength and frequency as time went on. Between 25 and 50 per cent of the children reported camouflaging their feelings, as they believed that they were not normal. They relied heavily on the support of their peer group, and found that the opportunity to discuss the death and re-tell the story helped them to cope with their feelings.

The anxiety, anger and depression which are characteristic of bereavement seemed overwhelming and produced fears for their own sanity. Some had enough self-control to keep all this to themselves, and deteriorating performance at school, poor concentration and memory, and what looked like sullen irritability were what showed on the surface. There is no doubt, then, that loss in adolescence can be devastating and can lead to ongoing emotional problems and difficulties with relationships if it is not helped at the right time. The needs are the same as in bereavement at any age, but it may not be the parent(s) who can fulfil them. A minister of religion, teacher, youth leader, family friend, godparent — someone the child is comfortable with and can talk to and discuss feelings and emotions, and who can be available to the child, can be invaluable. Where extra difficulties are apparent, or the grieving process seems unduly prolonged or stuck at one stage, it is worth getting skilled counselling. Cruse, or the local hospice, should be able to put the family in touch with someone trained to help. Skilled counselling at this time can help to stop difficulties experienced now going on into adult life.

The child facing death

When circumstances permit, and the family wants it, it is becoming more common nowadays for a terminally ill child to be nursed at home. This is not always possible if specialist care is not near at hand, but advances in some types of treatment, the provision of day hospitals, and the training of specialist community nurses, have made it an increasingly available option. When the child needs to be in hospital, the provision of accommodation for families, and liberal policies on visiting, mean that close contact can still be maintained.

How much to tell, and when, and to whom, involve difficult decisions, which clearly will vary from case to case. If there are other children in the family who will notice high degrees of distress and anxiety in their parents, or perhaps see the sick child as getting away with behaving badly, or being spoilt, or being the centre of everyone's attention, they will need explanations and reassurance. Brothers and sisters can be helped with their difficult feelings, including resentment and fear of loss of parental love, by being allowed to talk about them. It is also helpful if they are encouraged to take a full part in family affairs at the time of crisis, and are included in discussions. Jo-Ann Gyulay[25] points out that some of their difficulties can be alleviated if they are allowed to help parents, if their efforts to care for the sick child are praised, and if the hardships they endure are acknowledged. As far as they are able to and want to, they should go on clinic visits and become familiar with the hospital routine. If it is possible, space should be left for their concerns and interests too. If running them to and from clubs and hobby activities is too much for weary and preoccupied parents, it is the kind of job that other relatives and friends will probably be happy to undertake.

The sick child will also need to have his fears and concerns attended to. In children under five years old, it is likely that his main anxieties will centre around separation from mother. If she is there to comfort and reassure, he may need nothing else in the way of emotional help. He may have only the vaguest concept of death, so there would be no point in attempting discussion.

In older children, there may be no awareness of the serious-ness of the illness or of the possibility of death. Unpleasant procedures and other immediate concerns are more likely to trouble them. Opinions are divided about the advisability of telling apparently unaware children that they are very sick and there is a chance that they will die. Most writers suggest that waiting for questions to be asked is the right approach; some, however, feel that a child may be afraid of death, *and* may be afraid to ask about it. Some children express the fear symboli-cally in stories or drawings, which may give a lead into discussion. Others may simply show distress and anxiety in their behaviour. In cases like these, family members and the care team need to be in good, close communication with each other, so that an informed decision can be made about what to say. They will then need to be ready to deal with the child's reactions. It is important that people have a clear idea of what to say about death (see page 91), and religion may have a significant part to play. Even if it does not, a loving and reassuring account, in which peacefulness is stressed, can be given. Parents should have access to a specially trained staff member who will help them with this if need be. Whether or not death is discussed with the child, the maintenance of close, loving and honest relationships, in which the child can feel secure, is the crucial factor.

14

Other kinds of loss

Any kind of major loss involves a period of upheaval and change. Established habits and patterns of living are challenged and may be thrown into disarray. There is a time of uncertainty. 'Someone keeps moving the goal posts,' was the neat way a patient put it recently.

However, not all the major losses in life come through death. There are other major 'exits' which can lead to a period of grief. Deep relationships can end in disaster, friends move far away, jobs can be lost, chronic illness can produce major life-changes. While bereavement by death often *feels* like loss of part of the self, accident or illness can *literally* rob us of part of the self. Loss of a job can take away part of our identity. Moving house, even if it's through choice, may take away friends, familiar places, a sense of belonging. These transitions are bound to cause disruption and distress, and may also result in grief. As in bereavement, in most cases the grief will run its course from shock through anger and depression, pining for the past, and finally letting go and resolution.

Sometimes losses are counterbalanced by the opening-up of new possibilities. The trauma of moving house, for example, may be offset by having a new community to engage in, and a new home to plan for, so that there are positive, forward-looking elements too. The old house may be rich in memories, but they are portable; tied to the person rather than the place.

When a move involves a very great deal of change, as from one country to another, or from a longtime family home to sheltered accommodation, there is need for a great deal of adjustment, and it can seem overwhelming. It may lead to chronic anxiety and depression. Much of the stress in the situation can be eased, however, if the new community contains some familiar elements and is felt to be friendly, and people from the old environment keep in contact, so that 'bridges' are made between the old life and the new. When the person moving is actively involved in planning for the move and making decisions, this also helps to retain a feeling of control. The characteristics of the person concerned, the pluses and minuses of the new house, and the amount of positive support and help received, will all have a significant part to play in determining whether the experience will be able to be used for personal growth, or will be the cause of lifelong mourning.

Through the painstaking work of researchers such as Colin Murray Parkes and Beverley Raphael, among others (see further reading), we now know many of the characteristics of people, and types of loss, which will influence outcome for good or bad. This ought to mean that it is possible to plan ahead to offset the worst effects of some kinds of loss, and to deal with all those who have suffered loss in a thoughtful and humane way, so that their whole future is not compromised. This body of knowledge can be used by individual people, by their friends and relatives, by professionals.

Some other sources of grief are less obvious, in that they are concerned with things which *failed* to happen, rather than those which once existed but have been lost. Failing to achieve a particular goal, longing for or engaging in a relationship which does not come to fruition, remaining childless. These can be difficult to come to terms with, as the loss has no reality outside the head and heart of the loser. Most people are able to reach a point where they can acknowledge that the longed-for object will now never be attained, and they have a period of grief and then let it go and move on to other things. Some are not able to do this, and may remain angry, bitter, grieving. They cannot find joy in what is, because they are wrapped up in what might have been. It is not unusual to find that there has been an earlier, unresolved grief in people who have such difficulties later. They can often be helped by some form of counselling or psychotherapy. It is certainly worth trying if the alternative is to remain 'stuck' in an unhappy state which sours life and relationships.

In the following sections of this chapter, bereavement and grief caused by events other than death are briefly explored. They are the loss of a job, loss engendered by chronic illness or disability, and loss of a significant relationship. Like death, they too can result in a period of mourning. As in loss by death, the personalities involved, events leading up to the loss and consequent upon it, and amount of support, will all have a part to play for better or worse. The chance to be prepared for the loss is also important. This is by no means a comprehensive list of types of loss, but more of a sample of some of the major types.

Losing a job

Work, whether it is in the form of paid employment, or some kind of regular, purposeful activity directed towards obtaining the necessities of life more directly, as in subsistence farming; whether it is concerned with basics like food, or more abstract tasks like the creation of pleasing objects, is universal. It is not just something we have to do in order to survive physically; it appears to be something we need to do to survive socially and psychologically.

The work we do tells us, and others, a great deal about who we are. It gives us a place in society, and thus aids a sense of belonging. It contributes to self-esteem and a sense of personal security. In our society today, work usually implies paid regular employment. Jahoda[26] has identified five broad categories of experience which are shared by the majority of those who participate in work, and which are socially and psychologically important: work requires regular activity; imposes a time-structure on its participants; provides the opportunity to engage in a collective purpose or effort, gives status and identity, and provides areas of social experience less emotionally charged than family life. Maslow talks about work providing safety, belonging, self-esteem, and self-actualization. Clearly, the loss of these important categories of experience will be significant and likely to lead to a period of grief and stress.

Jahoda's categories deserve further consideration. The value of regular activity and a time-structure will be immediately obvious to anyone who has had to live without them for any length of time. Having nothing in particular to do and all the time in the world to do it may seem like heaven in the short term, but it soon begins to take its toll of energy and purpose.

The opportunity to engage in a collective effort can provide a deep level of satisfaction for the participants. To share a sense of achievement with others helps to bind people together. To be part of the team is something so fundamentally pleasing to people that many will seek its opportunities outside work, in leisure and sporting activities.

Work also gives status and identity. 'What do you do for a living?' must be the most commonly asked question in a social encounter, after names have been exchanged. The answer gives an immediate clue to a lot more information about the other person, and it opens up possibilities for conversation. What someone does for a living is always interesting, either because it is familiar and provides a chance to share experiences, or because it is unfamiliar and gives an opportunity to hear about something new. It tells the listener how much or little he or she is likely to have in common with the other person, and places him or her in the social hierarchy.

A day-to-day experience which is sociable but not so emotionally charged as family life gives opportunities for satisfying but relatively undemanding social contact. It is usual for friendships to be based around work, and networks of social support.

When the answer to the question, 'What do you do?' is 'Nothing,' it is perhaps not surprising that the questioner may feel at a loss, and not know how to respond positively. There may be no common experiences to share, and what do you say to someone who has just denied you most of the usual social responses? We still tend to assume that other people will be in work, and are often at a loss when they fail to fit the mould, even when full employment has been a thing of the past for some years. There still seems to be a feeling that people 'ought' to work, and a readiness to blame the unemployed for their own plight. If someone really wants to work, the myth has it, somehow it would happen. Thus we distance ourselves from those who fall outside the range of 'normal' experience; they make us feel uncomfortable.

Taking all these factors into account, it is small wonder that losing a job can be a major source of stress and grief. It robs us of so much more than a pay packet although that too is often a very important part of the loss. When Holmes and Rahe[27] compiled their Social Readjustment Rating Scale, they began by asking a large number of people from several different cultures to rate life-events for the amount of discontinuity and need for adjustment they would cause. Losing a job ranks high on the list, particularly if it is through firing or lay-offs. As Jahoda has pointed out, to be robbed of the opportunity to work is not a simple matter, it can have far-reaching social and psychological consequences.

Since the 1930s, there has been a growing body of research on the effects of unemployment on health. Fortunately we do not nowadays see extreme poverty and consequent malnutrition as a sequel of unemployment but other health effects have been noted.

When a meat-processing factory in a small English town closed, the families of 129 workers (80 men and 49 women) had their health records checked[28]. An increase in ill-health was demonstrated, shown by increased consultation of general practitioners, and increased referral and attendance at hospital out-patient departments. The decline in health began when the management first began to intimate that production might have to stop, which was two years before it actually did, and the trend continued for two more years after closure, while the study went on.

Unemployment has also been linked with the suicide rate, increased risk of hospital admission (particularly psychiatric) and other manifestations of chronic stress. In 1978, Hill[29] identified three phases of psychological response to unemployment — shock, meaningless leisure and lowered self-esteem, and finally a broken state where anxiety and depression are not necessarily still present, but there are feelings of inferiority, submissiveness, and acceptance of one's new identity as a jobless person.

Several writers have suggested that losing a job can lead to a grief response, like any other form of loss. At the end of grieving, if it is accomplished, job searching will begin as energy and purposefulness return. If the search is not successful, enthusiasm will eventually inevitably give way to apathy, stagnation and frustration, and so begin a new cycle of disability.

It is important, however, to stress that these reactions are by no means universal. It is more likely that those people who are already vulnerable because of previously poor physical or mental health, or who lack family support, or for whom unemployment is a worse-than-average financial disaster, will be over-represented in the hospital admissions group. The pattern of response to unemployment is influenced by these and other factors. Having too much of one's life invested in one's job, so that everything else is relatively neglected, can also be a recipe for disaster if the job is lost. There is another side to the coin, too.

In a study reported in 1979 Kash[30] looked at the psychological and physical conditions in a group of low-skilled American workers before and after redundancy, and concluded that the employment conditions had had such a bad effect on the workers that losing their jobs was not such a big trauma, and had, if anything, improved health.

A further study in Britain looked at the workers in a closing steel works[31] where a 'small army' of redundancy counsellors was drafted in. They stressed the importance of family support, maintaining outside activities and interests, and active job seeking. Until new employment was found, the chance to do things there had never been time to do before was one positive feature, and some workers enjoyed the idea of 'turning over a new leaf'. In this particular case, they were not alone in losing a job, as all the jobs had gone. The factory managers knew the value of preparing the workforce for redundancy, and also made a point of formally thanking and saying goodbye to the workers. Each was given a piece of the last ingot to be smelted there, engraved with the name of the company, the dates during which the factory was in existence, and 'Pride and Dignity'. In all these ways, they had tried to prevent the anger and loss of self-esteem which can be a destructive feature of job-loss, and they seem to have had a measure of success.

As in any other loss, the need to disengage from the lost object and find, eventually, a new focus of interest and satisfaction, is crucial. When re-employment is not a realistic option, the worst effects of unemployment can be mitigated by family support, counselling, advice and information (from statutory and voluntary schemes) on leisure, job creation, retraining, benefits and practical help.[32] Companionship and stimulation are also important, as is the attempt to keep to a time-structured and organized routine. Jahoda's five broad categories of experience normally supplied by going to work, can be created outside of work. When someone is able to engage in regular activity, make a time-structure, engage in a collective effort and obtain satisfying social experiences, many of the worst effects of unemployment may be avoided.

When there is time to prepare in advance for redundancy or retirement, opportunities to look at things like projected income, possible expenses, and options concerning pensions, can all be helpful. They may serve, not only to take the fear of poverty out of the equation, but also to enhance the sense of control of one's life. A new phase to be planned for and taken charge of. Health programmes, and the considered use of leisure time can and should be planned and perhaps begun in advance of the job loss, to smooth the transition. This is the responsibility of the firm as well as the employee, but, where the firm lacks the will or resources to engage in such programmes, the individual should contact their local college of further education for information on courses. Preparation can take much of the stress from transitional life-events.

In all these ways, unemployment can have some of the sting taken out of it, and it need not be the threat to mental and physical health that it sometimes has been in the past. It may even be a new beginning, particularly if those around, and most especially those still fortunate enough to be in work, can get used to the idea of estimating a fellow human being's worth in terms other than paid work; and can learn to accept that the apathy sometimes seen in the unemployed (particularly in young people who have never been employed) is not innate laziness but a reaction to feelings of worthlessness. Moreover, it is a reaction which can be helped in some of the ways suggested, but will not usually respond to a negative or critical approach which only serves to lower self-esteem further. The way back may not be through looking for a job at first, but through allowing and encouraging the rebuilding of a sense of personal worth.

Serious illness and disability

Disability caused by an accident or illness is, like any other kind of major life-change, hard to take in all at once. When someone dies, it takes time to remember consistently that they are not there any more. Many aspects of life will be the same as they were before, and they will be what we are used to. The necessary changes have to be taken in bit by bit, as we come across them. There is also often a deep longing for the old familiar times, strong enough to overcome reality and reason, on occasions. People 'hear' a loved one's voice, 'see' him or her in the street, have vivid dreams, with the quality of reality, in which the lost one lives again. These things fade away with time, as a new way of living is learned, and the past left behind. We have to learn all these complicated things in a step-by-step way, and this includes how to be a single person again, or how to be a parent without a child, or how to be disabled. There are so many implications in all these things, and they will not all become apparent at once. For all these reasons, we learn to adapt slowly. However, death and the personal disaster of disability both present many urgent tasks in the early days, when it is hard for the shocked and bewildered person to concentrate and take in information. Often, people go through these times as if they are on automatic pilot, and it is easy for people around to assume that everything is going well and that the person is coping. A particularly striking example of how someone can appear to be coping in the early days of their disability was given by a man who had damaged one leg badly in an accident. He underwent a series of operations to try to save the leg, but finally it had to be amputated. He maintained a calm demeanour through it all, until the day his artificial leg came, when he suddenly went into a state of shock. He had managed to get by without facing reality up until then.

In the first weeks after an accident or illness, many things may conspire to keep reality at bay. Consciousness may be impaired by the event itself, or by the drugs or procedures used in treatment. Severe pain can be so preoccupying that no room is left for other thoughts. Parts of the body may be numb or immobilized. Enforced bed-rest can also distort the perception of time and events. Memory of this time is often very hazy and incomplete. During this time most people will be in hospital, and struggling with unfamiliar surroundings, faces, procedures and routines. Having to deal with all this new information may also prevent someone from getting to grips with themselves and their new situation. This phase is like the frozen immobility of early grief — the first reaction to overwhelming bad news.

In bereavement by death, practical details like funeral arrangements may help people over this stage, but coming to terms with disability may be quite different in timescale if the acute stage of the illness or the need for intensive care is prolonged. It is common, for example, for the care of serious spinal injuries to involve six weeks of total immobilization. At that stage, the future may be unclear to everyone. People sometimes seem to pass that time in a dream-like state, in which acceptance and adaptation cannot begin. After severe head injury, consciousness may be impaired for weeks and so adaptation cannot begin. New learning is not taking place. Eventually, when this time passes, the full extent of the current disability, and its implications for the future, must be faced. It is not uncommon for denial and disbelief to be experienced then — by relatives, as well as the disabled person. This period may be complicated by the uncertainty of the possible degree of recovery, which cannot always be fully known. Anger, particularly directed at the care team, may dominate other feelings. It is important for everyone to understand that this anger is part of the difficulty of accepting the hard truth, and wanting to rebel against it; it is no time to get angry in return, as it is vital that caring relationships are maintained. This is also often a time when people ask the same questions over and over again, perhaps hoping that one person will say something different and more positive. The anger and the demanding repetitive questions often mask deep-rooted fears for the future which need to be uncovered and explored.

A common fear is that aspects of the particular illness or disability will make the person unlovable. 'How can anyone love me with my ugly scar/colostomy bag/mastectomy/wheelchair/ inability to support my family/inability to make love to my wife/speech defect/loss of bladder control . . .?' Sometimes these fears are real, and the partner or close family member is repelled and made afraid. Where the relationship was not good before, acquired disability is unlikely to improve it. Sometimes, skilled help can overcome these problems, sometimes it cannot, and the worst fears of the sufferer may be realized — they will be abandoned. Mercifully, cases such as these are rare. Where there is appropriate support, information and practical back-up, families can be helped to face and deal with a loved one's disability, and everyone learns that love is not conditional. The person you love is not the scarred face or useless legs, nor is he/she the trappings of colostomy or dysfunctional bladder. These are real, but do not detract from the *personality* of the sufferer in the long run, if the right kind of help and support is given when it is needed.

Members of the care team, who may be hospital or community-based, will be able to offer more than information and practical assistance. Some, particularly social workers, clinical psychologists and certain specialist nurses, will have counselling skills. These skills are also being increasingly taught to others such as physiotherapists and occupational therapists. Often the initiative comes from the therapists themselves. They are aware that the way information is given may be crucial, and also that all their skilled efforts may come to nothing if emotional problems overwhelm their patients. In his book, *Psychological Care in Physical Illness*[33] Keith Nichols highlights the need for informational care, and the devastating effects of unrecognized and undealt-with anxiety. Increasingly, the skills to deal with these aspects of patient care are being taught. There are now specialist mastectomy counselling nurses and stoma care nurses, among others, whose job is to facilitate living with those particular kinds of loss. Others have undergone training in areas such as sexual functioning in the disabled. They are available not only to the person in their care, but to partners, family members and close friends.

Another positive change in care patterns is the case of the key worker, who will often, but not always, be a nurse and whose job is to keep in touch and liaise with other members of the team. Ideally, contact will be maintained for as long as it is needed, and can be reinstated in difficult times, even when things seem to have gone well for ages.

Sometimes, long after discharge from hospital, the danger that depression and apathy will overtake someone grappling with loss or disability, remains real. The energy and activity involved in settling someone back into the community, inevitably tends to wane after a while. People may feel very confident while in hospital, and be able to carry out necessary new skills with ease. The reality of having to carry out the same routine, perhaps every day, perhaps for ever, without the back-up of hospital facilities, can be very different. The tasks ahead may seem too much to be dealt with, and the sufferer may sink into helplessness. This often happens after a period when everything seemed to be going well, and there may be a reluctance to call in the care team, as it looks like failure. However, the truth is that the likelihood of depression will be well known to them, and they will also know that early intervention can prevent the situation worsening. If this mood is severe and prolonged, and accompanied by disturbances of sleep and appetite, it may need treatment with anti-depressant drugs. In most cases, however, skilled counselling and patience will help to overcome the depression, which is properly regarded as a normal phase of adjustment to significant loss. The sick or disabled person may be unable, at first, to share their feelings with those close to them, as they may fear to upset loved ones by revealing the depths of their own despair, or the main source of worry may be being a burden. A counsellor can help with this; once those feelings have been expressed to a professional listener, it may be easier to share them with others.

Gradually, people move towards accepting reality, and are able to get on with life as it is, rather than being preoccupied with grieving for the past. As depression lifts, people become more active, and begin to try out the new life and new ways of coping. Support by the family is an important factor, as is support for the family. No one should feel that they 'ought' to be able to cope with major transitions without help. Even the strongest and most positive individual may simply need information and guidance. The best care is based on close communication, and on decision-making and planning as a shared task between the patient, primary carers and professional back-up staff.

When the basic physical rehabilitation is complete, as far as it can be, and healing has taken place as much as it is going to, there still may be problems to be dealt with. When ongoing pain or mental problems remain, they can change people and change relationships in a fundamental way. Chronic pain can certainly change how people behave. Fortunately, in recent years, there has been a move away from treating pain with strong drugs and operations as a first line of attack. New-style pain clinics offer a variety of pain management regimes which do not dull consciousness or cause unpleasant side-effects. These clinics are usually attached to district hospitals, and patients can be referred to them by family doctors. Because they tend to concentrate on the management of pain, with the patient as an actively involved member of the team, they counteract the tendency to helplessness and apathy so often seen when pain is a long-term problem.

Groups of chronic pain sufferers have banded together in self-help organizations such as the Back Pain Association, and Arthritis Care. These groups can offer a great deal to members in terms of practical help and support, and can also act as pressure groups and agents for change, keeping the problems of their members in the public eye.

Other types of problems facing the relatives of those with acquired disability, as well as the sufferers themselves, are particularly hard to bear. Sometimes a disease has an unpredictable progression (multiple sclerosis is an example) and grief for the losses that come with it is not pinned to one traumatic event, but more diffuse and hard to deal with. In some conditions, such as Alzheimer's disease (presenile dementia) the body may look the same as ever, and there is no physical disability, but because it affects the brain, the person inside the familiar body becomes unrecognizable. Some kinds of stroke, head injury, mental illness and dementia can cause changes in personality and behaviour which are completely uncharacteristic of the well person. The new person who seems to inhabit the familiar body all or some of the time is often unloveable.

Relatives attempting to cope and come to terms with these things face a hard task. Should they get angry with unreasonable behaviour? How much can the sufferer help it? How should they be helping? All too often, relatives try to deal with these problems alone, and in some cases are driven to violence against the sick member, and are then riddled with feelings of guilt and inadequacy. Family support, rapid access to professional care staff, and schemes such as holiday relief are invaluable where there are long-term difficulties such as these. They depend on a good working relationship between the family and the liaison worker, who might be a community nurse or social worker. Where good communication is maintained, crises can often be prevented, and the family held together.

Like bereavement, acquired disability or chronic illness appears to rob us of the future. One future is taken away, perhaps, but not *the* future. It is easy to be overwhelmed by the enormity of the tasks involved in facing illness, but it need not be faced alone.

As well as the help available from trained professionals, there are increasing numbers of clubs and self-help groups starting up. They help to raise funds for support, and offer friendship and practical help to members. They tend to cater for specific illnesses or injuries such as strokes, arthritis, head and spinal injuries and multiple sclerosis. They will understand the particular needs of chronic sick and disabled people, as the central core of membership will be formed from people who have had personal experience of it. People sometimes fear to join such groups, feeling that they might be full of sad people sitting around swapping symptoms. In my experience, this is far from the case. The groups with which I have been associated have been lively and dynamic, and full of people determined to do something positive to help themselves and others. Some have transformed the lives of sufferers from disease or disability, and their close family, and given hope. Because they are independent of the medical and social-work professions they help to counterbalance feelings of over-dependence on professional care, and thus to restore self-esteem. Contact your local health practitioner or civic information centre for the addresses of these organizations.

Loss of relationships

When we enter into a close relationship with another person the expectation is that there will be mutual cherishing. The self-esteem of each person will be enhanced by being loved; loneliness will be abolished; help and comfort will be available. The breakdown of such a relationship is bound to cause distress, whether it has been formalized as a marriage or not. Close, stable relationships where there is good communication are less likely to break down than those in which there is already a degree of conflict, so a breakdown is often preceded by a period of unhappiness and difficulty. The effects of being rejected and alone are often felt to be severe enough to keep people together in an unhappy relationship. The loss of intimacy and social support, and the effect on self-esteem of being rejected, are experienced as very threatening. Statistics tend to show that those people who find themselves alone again after a marriage or similar relationship, are more prone to clinical depression, alcoholism and attempted suicide than those in stable relationships. Loss of contact with children, or the stresses of bringing up children alone, and financial hardship, may all be additional complicating factors.

Even when the break-up has been preceded by a long period of conflict, so that when it comes it is felt as a relief, the aftermath is often like bereavement by death. The shock, pining, anger and depression are there, as is the guilt and the feeling of 'if only . . .'. Sometimes, circumstances can make it more painful. To be rejected by someone you love, perhaps because he or she has found someone they prefer, can bring a feeling of humiliation; you have been weighed in the balance and found wanting. Even if logic tells you that your ex-partner was the wrong person or a bad person, it was your choice — your bad choice. Confidence is often shaken. The break-up may make friends and relatives feel threatened in their relationships too, so that expected sources of support may not be available. Sadly, the experiences of widows and widowers, who may find that people avoid them or fail to include them in social invitations, tend to be echoed by the divorced and separated.

Those who enter into close, loving relationships tend to have high expectations of each other. As time and circumstance produce changes, there is a need for people to be flexible and adaptable, and yet remain stable. The need to adapt to the other person and yet not compromise important aspects of the self, is a tricky path to negotiate. A study carried out by R.M. Pierce showed that almost 50 per cent of couples reported difficulties associated with housing, money, family, religion and sex. Not all those difficulties lead to breakdown, but they can be additional burdens on a couple struggling to maintain a loving relationship. The idea that having children will help to hold together a relationship in difficulties is false, and yet it continues to be attempted as a solution.

Studies have demonstrated a number of trends in marital breakdown. Marrying young is a high risk factor for breakdown. There are two peak times for breakdown to occur. One is very early indeed, after between one and two years after marriage. Either the marriage was a mistake, or the difficult settling-down period in the relationship failed to be resolved. Still today the image of romantic love as all important in the marital relationship is emphasized, and the importance of compatibility, friendship, and working at the difficulties, are brushed under the carpet. Leaving the success of marriage to love and chance is obviously risky; perhaps the idea of education for marriage, and pre-marriage counselling, will one day become established, and some of these casualties will be avoided. However, as Dominian has pointed out[35] there is no substitute for the continuous preparation for future life of the child at home. It is at home that the child will begin to learn about marriage, from the relationship of its parents. What it learns in those early years will shape its ideas of marriage. There is a large body of evidence which suggests that people from broken homes have an increased risk that their own marriage will suffer, and an increased likelihood of difficulty with personal relationships. Not only will they have grown up with a bad model of marriage, but disharmony and conflict between parents can have a devastating effect on a developing personality and on feelings of security. Thus, the prevention of marital disharmony in one generation will influence marriages in the next.

While the early years show the highest incidence of breakdown, marriages or other long-term stable relationships can also disintegrate in later years. The reasons for this are not well understood, and a number of factors may be operating. People change as they mature; sometimes changes in needs and expectations can drive a couple apart. Years spent in child-rearing come to an end, and if the children have been the main bond and point of communication, breakdown can occur when they leave home. Many other life-changes put a marriage under stress. It is relatively unusual for couples to seek help until the problem has become severe, and sometimes by then the gaps between them are unbridgeable. Early intervention by organizations providing marriage guidance services needs to be encouraged.

If, however, breakdown is inevitable, the broken family will need the same kind of support, and will often show the same patterns of grief and be at the same kinds of risk, as those bereaved by death. Of course, there will be individual variations. Bitterness and conflict between separated parents will have a bad effect on children; maintaining a civil or even friendly contact, with children having access to both parents, tends to mitigate the effects. Those with vulnerable personalities, poor family and social support, and who are put in a bad financial position, will tend to be at extra risk in terms of health and emotional adjustment, and they should be the groups at which counselling and extra support is targeted. Once the relationship is over, it is too late for blame. The focus of attention should be on rescuing the casualties and helping to prevent the disaster becoming an ongoing or lifelong tragedy, just as in any other kind of major loss.

Epilogue

At the beginning of this book, the question, 'What are we to make of the losses we encounter in various forms from early in life?' was posed. It could equally well have asked what the losses make of us.

Losses which go on to become life-long tragedies have certain characteristics, such as suddenness, associated trauma, untimeliness. Concurrent circumstances also have a part to play for better or worse — things like the presence or absence of social support, dramatic financial problems resulting from loss, and the provision of care. Finally, there is the person who has suffered the loss. If they are already prone to anxiety, physically ill or disabled, dependent by nature, or made vulnerable by earlier unresolved sorrows, they may have extra difficulty in adapting to change. Dozens of pieces of careful research have enabled these potentially hazardous factors to be identified. We are now able to predict who is likely to be at risk, and the circumstances under which poor outcome is likely to arise. This means that we have the theoretical knowledge necessary to enable us to target resources where they are needed. To some extent, some of the needs of bereaved people are being met by self-help groups such as the Stillbirth and Neonatal Death Society, the Compassionate Friends and Cruse. These organizations provide friendship and practical help, and, in some cases, expert counselling.

Bereavement counsellors are also being trained in increasing numbers under the auspices of the hospice movement. In addition to the provision of counselling training for lay people, there are courses for nurses on various aspects of death and bereavement. The compassionate concern felt by some people through the ages, for those who have suffered loss, has been underpinned by expert research and writing.

While some fear of death will probably remain with us, because it has unknown elements and because it takes those we love away from our immediate physical world, it may be that we are beginning to move away from a fear so intense that it can cut the newly-bereaved off from other people. The additional isolation and loneliness reported by bereaved people when others keep away from them is surely a consequence of ignorance and unpreparedness. Nowadays, increasing numbers of people, both professional and laymen, have the opportunity to learn about death and bereavement. The taboo on such matters is beginning to be lifted. There is still a long way to go, however, before education about death is included as a routine part of learning about life.

It is still largely a matter of chance whether some people get the right kind of help — or any help — in bereavement. This is dictated by where someone lives, whether the GP is aware of self-help groups and other sources of aid, how sensitive and aware hospital staff are, and so on. Slowly, though, the network of informed people is spreading.

The chance of coping well with loss, and being able to grow because of it, can be enhanced in other ways. Practical and conceptual preparation for one's own death, preparation for the possibility of being left alone; the maintenance of good, mutually supportive relationships extending beyond the immediate family; being able to cope on your own even while you do not have to — all these things can be sources of strength when the time comes.

Clearly, having a number of loving friends rather than one person in whom all your love is invested, protects anyone from the worst effects of loss. Keeping a balance and variety among the concerns in your life is also healthier in the long term. Someone who feels that all is lost if unemployment comes, or the children leave home, or physical changes reduce attractiveness, will have been programmed to be at risk because they have put too many psychological 'eggs' in one basket. We are versatile, stretchable beings, and seem to function best when we are not over-concerned with any one thing or person.

A belief system of some kind, not necessarily Christian, or even religious, in the conventional sense, is also armour against feelings of hopelessness and helplessness. These things often need working at as they do not necessarily come to order at times of crisis, but are best attended to *now*.

We do not need to become morbidly preoccupied with death in order to face it and its consequences calmly, and with hope, but we do need to give it due attention at some time. Like all of life's business, thought and planning make it easier than trusting in luck to get us through. Then, whether it is a matter of facing loss ourselves, or dealing, without fear or embarrassment, with someone else who has been bereaved, we will be better equipped. Not that being better equipped will take away the pain — the necessary pain — of loss, but it will prevent the addition of extra pain and grief, and should help to prevent the prolonging of mourning. Like many other psychologists and counsellors, I have listened to and spoken with large numbers of people who have been unduly hurt by being bereaved. Some of them were children when they suffered loss, and no one thought to explain things to them or listen to their fears. It was thought that they did not understand, and would get over it. Some of them wondered, as many children do, if it was all caused by something they did. With no one to reassure them, that feeling that they had done a bad thing, or were bad themselves, stayed with them, and sometimes caused great unhappiness later in life. Some of the bereaved were the capable ones in the family. Everyone turned to them in the crisis, and they were so busy helping all and sundry, and organizing things that no one else felt capable of, that they had no time for their own feelings. Feelings not acknowledged and dealt with do not go away; they are filed in the tray marked 'pending'. Some of the bereaved had complicated emotions about the deceased, which they perhaps could not express in their lifetime for one reason and another, and felt guilty about expressing after the death. These unexpressed feelings cannot be let go until something or someone helps the process. There are numerous other examples of how grief can be badly handled, and be worsened and prolonged because of it. The business of helping someone to unravel and explore their grief, and to come out from under its shadow at last, can be deeply rewarding, but I would rather not have to do it. So much of that suffering is unnecessary, preventable. Most bereaved people are hurt by others — not deliberately, but in ignorance, fear and superstition. The increasing availability of information from the media of education and communication is making its mark. Professional and lay people are becoming better-informed, and this can only be to the good of us all.

Loss touches us all. Its effects touch us all. We cannot afford not to be educated about it. If this book has encouraged its readers to do some thinking on their own behalf, and to feel better able to reach out to those in need of comfort, it will have done its work.

Useful addresses

When writing to any of these organizations, please enclose a stamped, addressed envelope for your reply.

United Kingdom

British Humanist Association (non-religious funeral literature and advice), 13 Prince of Wales Terrace, London W8 5PG Tel: 01-937-2341.

Compassionate Friends (network of bereaved parents offering friendship and understanding to others), The National Secretary, Compassionate Friends, 6 Denmark Street, Bristol BS1 5DQ Tel: 0272 292778. Some branches of Cruse also have parent groups.

Cruse (the national organization for the widowed and their children), Cruse House, 126 Sheen Road, Richmond, Surrey TW9 1UR Tel: 01-940-4818.

Foundation for the Study of Infant Deaths (information, support, reassurance, research in cot death cases) 15 Belgrave Square, London SW1X 8PS Tel: 01-235-1721/0965.

The Marie Stopes Clinic (for women who need emotional help after abortion), Tel: 01-388-2585.

The Miscarriage Association (offers help and support), 18 Stoneybrook Close, West Bretton, Wakefield WF4 4TP Tel: 0924-264579.

National Association of Widows (information and advice), H.Q.
Office, 54-57 Allison Street, Digbeth, Birmingham B5 5TH
Tel 021-643-8348.

SAFTA (Support After Termination of the Foetus Association
— for women who have had abortions because of foetal
abnormality) 22 Upper Woburn Place, London WC1 0EP
Tel: 01-388-1382.

Stillbirth and Neonatal Death Society (help and befriending),
28 Portland Place, London W1N 4DE Tel: 01-436-5881.

USA

American Humanists, 7 Harwood Drive, Amerst, New York NY
10028.

Bereavement and Loss Centre, 170e Eighty Third Street, New
York, NY 10028.

Compassionate Friends, 2131 Chapel Road, Birmingham, Ala-
bama 35226.

Pregnancy and Infant Loss Centre, 1415 East Wayzata Boule-
vard, Suite 22, Wayzata MN55391.

Widowed Persons Service, NRTA — AARP, 1909 K Street,
NW Washington DC 20049.

Australia

Compassionate Friends, Rear 205 Blackburn Road, Syndal,
Victoria 3149.

Humanist Society of Western Australia, Box T 1799 GPO,
Perth 6001.

The National Association of Civilian Widows, 239 Gregory
Terrace, Perth 6000, Western Australia.

Perth SANDS (Stillbirth and Neonatal Death Society), Room G9, Agnes Walsh House, Bagot Road, SUBIACO, Western Australia.

The Study of Infant Death Association of NSW, Box 172, St Ives, Sydney 2075, New South Wales.

New Zealand

National Children's Health Research — Cot Death Division, 5 Clonbern Road, PO Box 28-177, Auckland 5 Tel: 548 597.

New Zealand Humanists, 6 Mona Road, Wellington 5.

North Shore Bereaved Friends, 71 Juniper Bay, Auckland.

Widows and Widowers Association, PO Box 12-160, Wellington.

Addresses for organizations offering help and advice on specific illnesses and injuries can be obtained from your health practitioner.

Further reading

1   *Who Wants to Think About Dying?* Cruse - Bereavement Care, 126 Sheen Road, Richmond, Surrey TW9 1UR

2   *Bereavement*: Studies of grief in adult life, Colin Murray Parkes, Penguin (1972).

3   'The Harvard Study', in *Bereavement*, C.M. Parkes, Penguin (1972).

4   'Parents' responses to the death of adult children from accidents and cancer: A comparison (draft), in *Bereavement*, Colin Murray Parkes (1972)

5   *After Suicide*. S.E. Wallace. John Wiley (1973)

6   Look to the Living - Easing the Pain of the Aftermath of Suicide. Paul Lodge. *Social Work Today* Vol. 11 No.29 25.3.80 p.10-12.

7   *A Grief Observed*, C.S. Lewis, Faber and Faber (1961)

8   *Living with Loss*, Liz McNeill Taylor, Fontana (1983)

9   *In the Springtime of the Year*, Susan Hill, Hamish Hamilton (1974)

10   'Responding to the Bereaved: an analysis of helping statements', M Davidowitz and R. D. Myrick, *Death Education* 8, 1–10 (1984)

11   'Preventive intervention with the bereaved', Beverley Raphael, *Archives of General Psychiatry* 34:1450–1454, (1977)

12   'Evaluation of a bereavement service.' Colin Murray Parkes, *Journal of Preventive Psychiatry* 2: 197–188 (1981)

13   'Nobody Told Me' C. Simpson, *Nursing Mirror* 9 Nov. 1985 pxi

14   *Relaxation: Modern techniques for stress management*, Sandra Horn, Thorsons (1986)

15   'Assisting the bereaved', J. L. Schulman and J. L. Rehm, *Journal of Paediatrics* 102, 6 992–998 (1983)

16   'Living through grief', J. Emerson, *Nursing Mirror* 9 Nov. 1985 p. ii-vii

17   'Pathological grief in doctors' wives', E. Harari, *British Medical Journal* 282 p.33-34 (1981)

18   *Beginnings: A book for widows*, Betty Jane Wylie, Unwin (1986)

19   *The Anatomy of Bereavement*, Beverley Raphael, Hutchinson (1984)

20   *Death and Dying: A quality of life*, P.F. Pegg and E. Metze (eds), Pitman (1981)

21   *Acute Grief and the Funeral*, U.R. Pine (eds.) Springfield Illinois (R. Fulton p.73) 1976

22   *Cider with Rosie*, L. Lee, Penguin Books (1962)

23   *On Death and Dying*, Elisabeth Kübler-Ross, Tavistock Publications, (1970)

24   'Teenagers coping with sibling deaths: Some implications for school counsellors', *The School Counsellor*, Nov. 1983

25 *The Dying Child*, Jo-Ann Gyulay, McGraw Hill (1978)

26 *Employment and Unemployment*, M. Jahoda, Cambridge University Press (1982)

27 'The social readjustment rating scale', T.H. Holmes and R.H. Rahe, *Journal of Psychosomatic Research* 11 213–218, (1967)

28 'Job-loss and family morbidity: A study of a factory closure', N. Beale and S. Nethercott, *Journal of the College of General Practitioners* (1985)

29 'The psychological impact of unemployment', M.J. Hill, *New Society* (19th January 1978)

30 'Changes in mental health status associated with job loss and retirement', S.V. Kash in *Stress and Mental Disorder*, (J. Barret et al (eds), Raven Press (1978)

31 'Redundancy: Just the push I needed', T Burbury, *Health Service Journal*, 15 May 1986

32 *Redundancy: How to Cope with the Psychological and Practical Problems*, Theresa Crowley and Chris Bainton, Turnstone Press (1985)

33 *Psychological Care in Physical Illness*, Keith A. Nichols, Croom Helm (1984)

34 R.M. Pierce *Sociological Review* 1963

35 Marital Breakdown J. Dominian Pelican (1969)

These are not referred to in the text, but may prove useful.

What To Do When Someone Dies (E. Rudinger (ed) (1978)) published by the Consumers' Association has practical and legal information.

Bereavement: What to expect and how to be helpful. Available from MIND, 22 Harley Street, London W1N 2ED

Form FB29 from DHSS Offices, 'Help when Someone Dies', a guide to Social Security Benefits.

Also recommended

To Live Again, Catherine Marshall, Fontana (1967)

Begin Again: A book for women alone, Margaret Torrie, J. M. Dent (1970)

Through Grief: The bereavement journey, Elizabeth Collick, Darton, Longman & Todd (1986)

Index

*All in *Death and Dying: A* ·
  Quality of Life, P.F. Peff and
  E. Metze (Eds.) p. 122.